Book One

Essentials of Reading & Writing English

A Basic English Literacy Program

Judith S. Rubenstein • Janet M. Gubbay

National Textbook Company
a division of NTC *Publishing Group* • Lincolnwood, Illinois USA

To our husbands,
Howard S. Rubenstein and
Jacob D. Gubbay,
whose encouragement and support
made this possible

1990 Printing

Published by National Textbook Company, a division of NTC Publishing Group.
© 1989 by NTC Publishing Group, 4255 West Touhy Avenue,
Lincolnwood (Chicago), Illinois 60646-1975 U.S.A.
All rights reserved. No part of this book may be reproduced, stored
in a retrieval system, or transmitted in any form or by any means,
electronic, mechanical, photocopying, recording or otherwise, without
the prior permission of NTC Publishing Group.
Manufactured in the United States of America.

0 ML 9 8 7 6 5 4 3 2

Contents

Preface

Essentials of Reading and Writing English is a three-book series that offers students the opportunity to develop basic reading and writing skills in English. In addition, the material in these books will help students to improve their pronunciation as they become familiar with the sounds of English and the ways in which these sounds correspond to the written language. The three books in this series may be used independently or as a set by students of English as a first or second language who want to acquire basic reading and writing skills in English.

Book One presents the basic skills needed to read and write English. Step-by-step, students will learn the following:

- the alphabet in print, script, and book type
- one-syllable, three-letter, short-vowel words
- sentences composed of these words, such as *Kim can run*
- related sight words, such as *live, have, do,* and *me*
- life skills information, such as personal identification, numbers, time, colors, and idioms

All the lessons in Book One are presented using a format similar to the formats used in newspapers, magazines, mail, and books. The lines and spaces provided for students to write in are a standard size, like those found on typical forms at a bank, doctor's office, school, employment agency, or government office. The reading passages in the book reflect adult responsibilities and real-life situations within the limits of the lesson vocabulary.

Essentials of Reading and Writing English teaches students to read English using a phonetic approach because English is a phonetic language: all the words in the English language are formed from a combination of the twenty-six letters of the alphabet, and the sounds of these letters are limited and predictable. Using Book One, after learning only one sound for each of the twenty-six letters (twenty-one consonants and five vowels), students will be able to predict, read, and write over two thousand three-letter, short-vowel words and syllables. For example:

				Words	Syllables
h	a	s		has	mis
b	e	g		hat	seg
p	i	n		beg	sen
c	o	b	=	bet	han
r	u	t		pig	hab
m		l		pin	pol
s		c		cob	rec

$(21 \times 5 \times 21)$

Book Two of the series includes two-syllable, short-vowel words and sentences, blends, and related sight words. Book Three covers long-vowel words and sentences, special sounds, and related sight words.

Essentials of Reading and Writing English, with its clear format and easy-to-follow approach, simplifies the task of learning to read, write, and pronounce English. We have grouped words into meaningful patterns and provided a means of building essential reading and writing skills in English by presenting material in small, easily mastered increments. At the same time, the series offers mastery of a very complex curriculum. After completing Book One, students will have learned to

- read and write the alphabet
- read and pronounce hundreds of sound words
- predict the sounds of hundreds of additional short-vowel syllables
- read, pronounce, and write twenty-eight basic sight words

By combining the phonetic approach with the memorization of several vital sight words, students will have learned to read and write important examples of the following grammatical forms:

- present tense of the verb *to be*
- subject, object, and possessive pronouns
- types of sentences, including declarative, interrogative, imperative, exclamatory, compound, conditional, future tense, past tense, comparative, idiomatic, and quotation

Through using the three books in the *Essentials of Reading and Writing English* series, students will experience increased self-confidence and find success and pleasure in learning to read and write English.

Judith S. Rubenstein and Janet M. Gubbay

Acknowledgments

I want to express my gratitude to those persons and teachers in the field of education who have had the greatest influence on me: Dr. John B. Carroll, Roy Edward Larsen Professor of Educational Psychology, Emeritus, and former Director of the Laboratory for Research in Instruction, Harvard Graduate School of Education, and Dr. Fletcher G. Watson, Henry Lee Shattuck Professor of Education, Emeritus, Harvard Graduate School of Education, both of whom inspired and guided my graduate work; Eloise Gredler who, in her home-school, demonstrated to me the power of phonics for teaching reading; my students, who stimulated me to create materials that could help them, and on whom I tested the lessons in these books; Rebecca Rauff, ESL/EFL Editor, National Textbook Company, who so carefully and skillfully edited the manuscript; and finally to Janet M. Gubbay, my co-author, who first suggested we undertake to write this series and who has been a tireless, creative, and ideal partner since the beginning.

These volumes could not have been realized, however, without the support of my family. I am especially grateful to my husband, Howard S. Rubenstein, for his enthusiasm for this project from the start and for many helpful suggestions; to my daughter, Emily, who provided the draft illustrations for the manuscript; to all four of my children, Emily, Adam, Jennifer, and John, for their overall sense of humor and cooperation; to both my mother, Martha K. Selig, and my father, the late Dr. Kalman Selig, whose love of books and learning has been my ultimate teacher.

Judith S. Rubenstein

UNIT ONE:
The Alphabet

In Chapters 1 and 2, you will read and write

▶ shapes of letters

▶ the alphabet

You will learn the six forms of each letter:

	book type	print	script
lower-case letters	**a**	a	a
capital letters	**A**	A	A

CHAPTER 1:
Shapes of Letters

MATCH LEFT TO RIGHT $\longrightarrow$

Match one, left to right:

Example:

1.

5.

2.

6.

3.

7.

4.

8.

Match three, left to right:

Example:

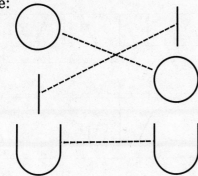

1.

3.

2.

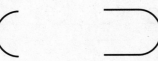

4.

CIRCLE AND WRITE

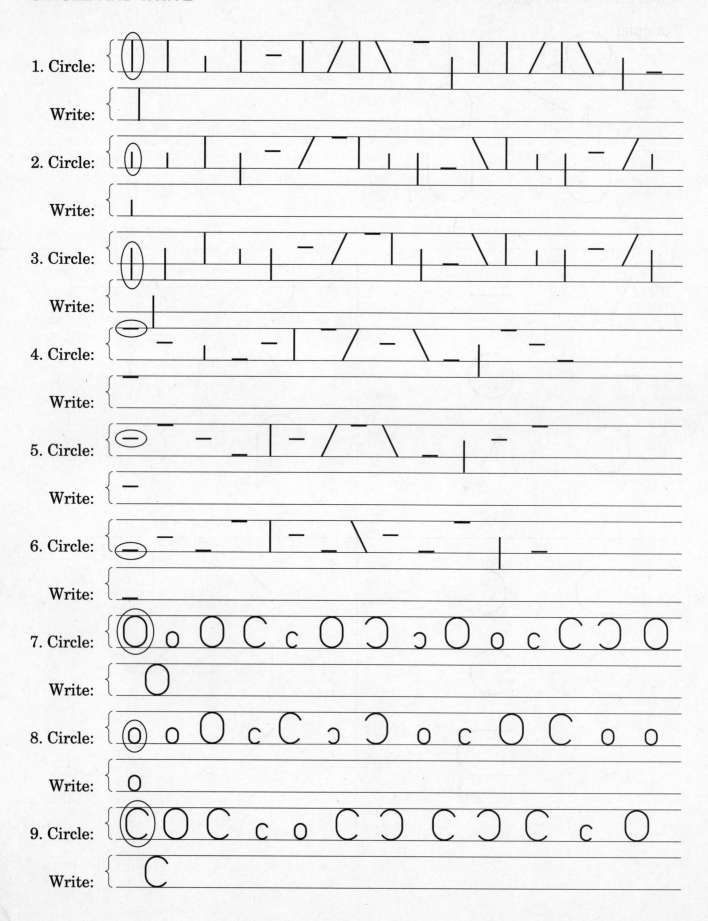

10. Circle: ⓒ c o C c o O u c o c u

Write: C

11. Circle: ⊘ \ \ | | \ ⎯ / \ | /

Write: /

12. Circle: ⊘ \ \ ⎯ | ⎯ \ ⎯ | \ |

Write: \

13. Circle: ⊙ ⊃ c o ⊃) ⊃ c ⊃ o c ⊃

Write: ⊃

14. Circle: ⊙) C)) ⊃ o) C))

Write:)

15. Circle: Ⓤ U u c U C) U O C U

Write: U

16. Circle: Ⓤ u c U o u ⊃ u u c U

Write: U

17. Circle: ⋒ ⋒ o o U ⋒ c ⋒ ⊃ U ⋒ O

Write: ⋒

18. Circle: Ⓓ ⊃ O c ⊃ ⊃ c ⊃ u ⊃)

Write: ⊐

CHAPTER 2:

The Alphabet

ALPHABET SUMMARY CHART 1: PRINT

This chart shows all 26 upper-case (capital) and lower-case letters of the English alphabet.

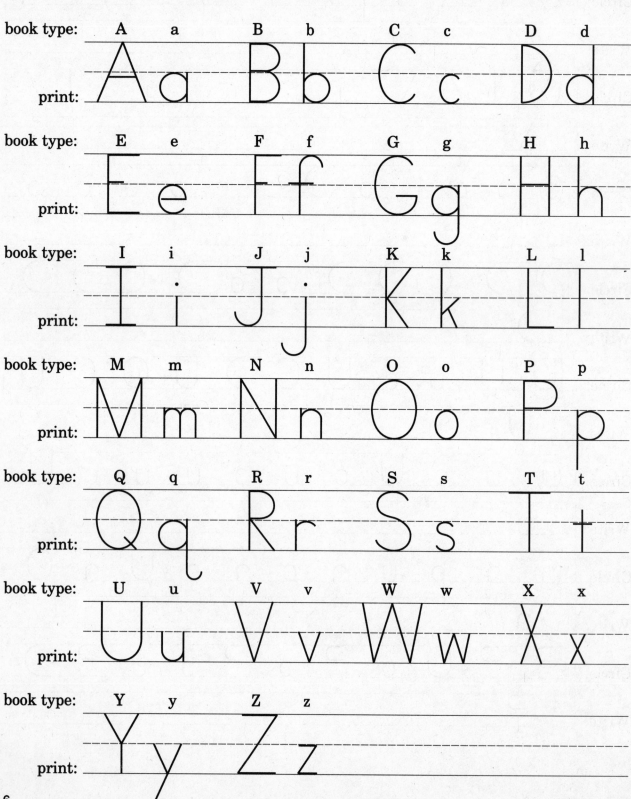

book type: A   a   B   b   C   c   D   d

print:

book type: E   e   F   f   G   g   H   h

print:

book type: I   i   J   j   K   k   L   l

print:

book type: M   m   N   n   O   o   P   p

print:

book type: Q   q   R   r   S   s   T   t

print:

book type: U   u   V   v   W   w   X   x

print:

book type: Y   y   Z   z

print:

ALPHABET SUMMARY CHART 2: SCRIPT

This chart shows all 26 upper-case (capital) and lower-case letters of the English alphabet.

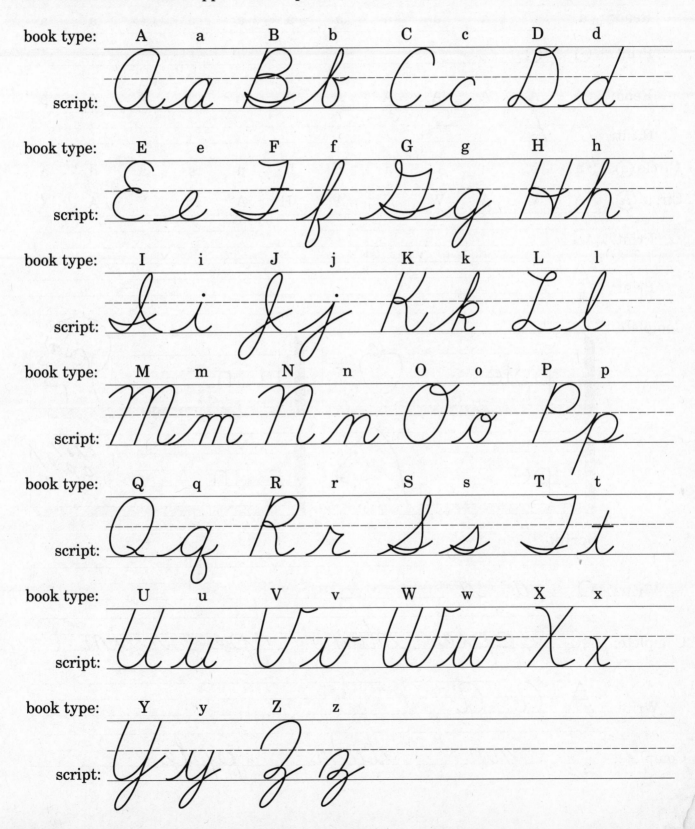

a a _a_
A A _A_

ă = apple
ā = ape

apple

Print

Read: a   a   a   a   a   a   a   a   a   a   a   a

Print: a   a   a   a

Read: A   A   A   A   A   A   A   A   A   A   A   A

Print: A   A   A   A

Circle ⓐ: a   o   e   u   a   c   b   a   s   a   d   a

Circle Ⓐ: A   V   A   W   N   A   H   A   M   Y   A   X

Print: a

Print: A

Complete:

apple

man

ape

rain

Script

Write: a = _a   a   a   a_

Complete: _apple   man   ape   rain_

Write: A = _a   a   a   a_

Complete: _Ann   Adam   Apple_

b b *ƀ*
B B *ℬ*

bus

Print

Read: b   b   b   b   b   b   b   b   b   b   b   b

Print: { b   b   b   b

Read: B   B   B   B   B   B   B   B   B   B   B   B

Print: { B   B   B   B

Circle ⓑ:   b   d   h   b   g   t   a   b   p   d   b   q

Circle Ⓑ:   B   D   P   B   E   S   B   H   K   R   B   P

Print: { b

Print: { B

Complete:

bus

baby

bed

cab

Script

Write: { b = *ƀ   ƀ   ƀ   ƀ*

Complete: { *bus baby bed cab*

Write: { B = *ℬ   ℬ   ℬ   ℬ*

Complete: { *Betty Ben Bed Bus*

c c *c*
C C C

ca ⎤
co ⎬ k =   can
cu ⎭   cot
              cup

ce ⎤
ci ⎬ s =   cereal
              city

can

Print

Read: c   c   c   c   c   c   c   c   c   c   c   c

Print: C   C   C   C

Read: C   C   C   C   C   C   C   C   C   C   C   C

Print: C   C   C   C

Circle ⓒ:   c   d   a   c   o   u   a   c   e   o   d   c

Circle Ⓒ:   C   O   D   C   G   Q   O   C   D   G   C   G

Print: C

Print: C

Complete:

can

clock

car

circle

Script

Write: C = C C C C

Complete: can clock car circle

Write: C = C C C C

Complete: Can Carl Chen

d d d
D D D

dollar

Print

Read: d d d d d d d d d d d d

Print: { d d d d

Read: D D D D D D D D D D D D

Print: { D D D D

Circle d: d a b d b a q d p b p a

Circle D: D B P R O D C P O D R C

Print: { d

Print: { D

Complete:

dollar

dog

doctor

bed

Script

Write: { d = d d d d

Complete: { dollar dog doctor bed

Write: { D = D D D D

Complete: { Dollar Don Din Dang

e e *e*

E E Ɛ

ĕ = egg

ē = teeth   egg

Print

Read: e   e   e   e   e   e   e   e   e   e   e   e

Print: { e e e e

Read: E   E   E   E   E   E   E   E   E   E   E   E

Print: { E E E E

Circle e: e   c   o   e   u   e   n   a   e   c   d   e

Circle E: E   F   E   T   E   I   E   F   E   N   H   E

Print: { e

Print: { E

Complete:

egg

bed

web

teeth

Script

Write: { e = *e   e   e   e*

Complete: { *egg bed web teeth*

Write: { E = *Ɛ   Ɛ   Ɛ   Ɛ*

Complete: { *Egg Emily Edward Ellen*

fish

Print

Read: f   f   f   f   f   f   f   f   f   f   f   f

Print: f f f f

Read: F   F   F   F   F   F   F   F   F   F   F   F

Print: F F F F

Circle f: f   t   g   k   h   f   t   d   f   b   f   d

Circle F: F   E   F   T   F   Z   E   E   F   I   L   F

Print: f

Print: F

Complete:

fish

fork

fan

cuff

Script

Write: f = f f f f

Complete: fish fork fan cuff

Write: F = F F F F

Complete: Frank Fanny Fish Fork

g g *g*
G G *G*

ga		gas
go }	g =	got
gu		gum
ge }	j =	gem
gi		ginger

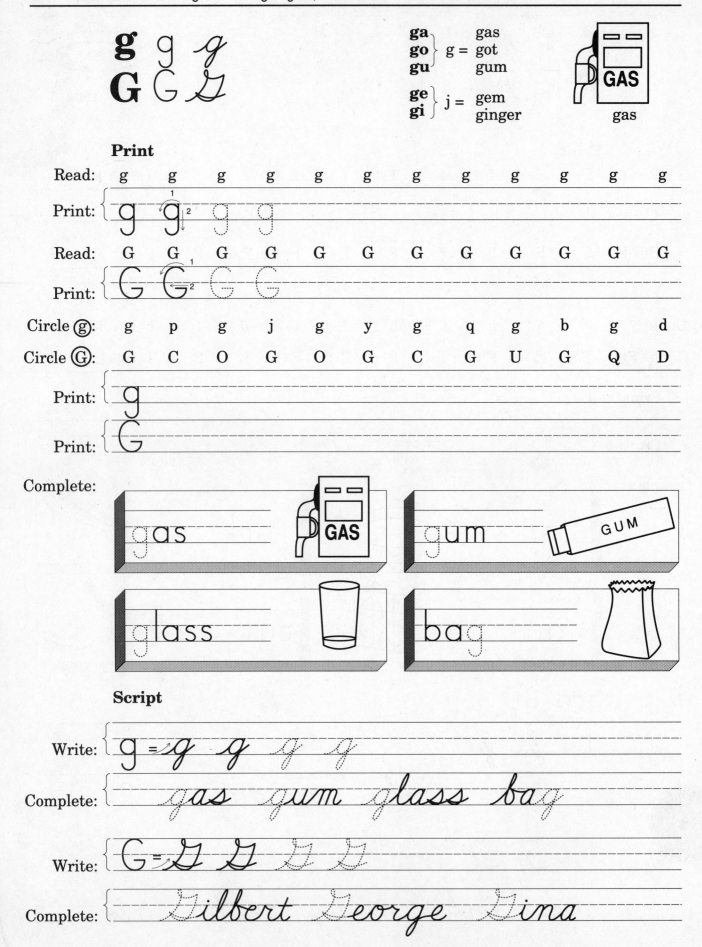

GAS

gas

Print

Read: g g g g g g g g g g g g

Print: g g g g

Read: G G G G G G G G G G G G

Print: G G G G

Circle ⓖ: g p g j g y g q g b g d

Circle Ⓖ: G C O G O G C G U G Q D

Print: g

Print: G

Complete:

gas — GAS

gum — GUM

glass

bag

Script

Write: g = g g g g

Complete: gas gum glass bag

Write: G = G G G G

Complete: Gilbert George Gina

h h *h*
H H *H*

hat

Print

Read: h   h   h   h   h   h   h   h   h   h   h   h

Print: h   h   h   h

Read: H   H   H   H   H   H   H   H   H   H   H   H

Print: H   H   H   H

Circle ⓗ: h   b   n   h   d   h   n   h   b   p   h   g

Circle Ⓗ: H   N   H   M   H   Y   H   A   H   W   X   H

Print: h

Print: H

Complete:

hat

horse

hand

house

Script

Write: h = *h   h   h   h*

Complete: *hat horse hand house*

Write: H = *H   H   H   H*

Complete: *Howard Henry Hang Hat*

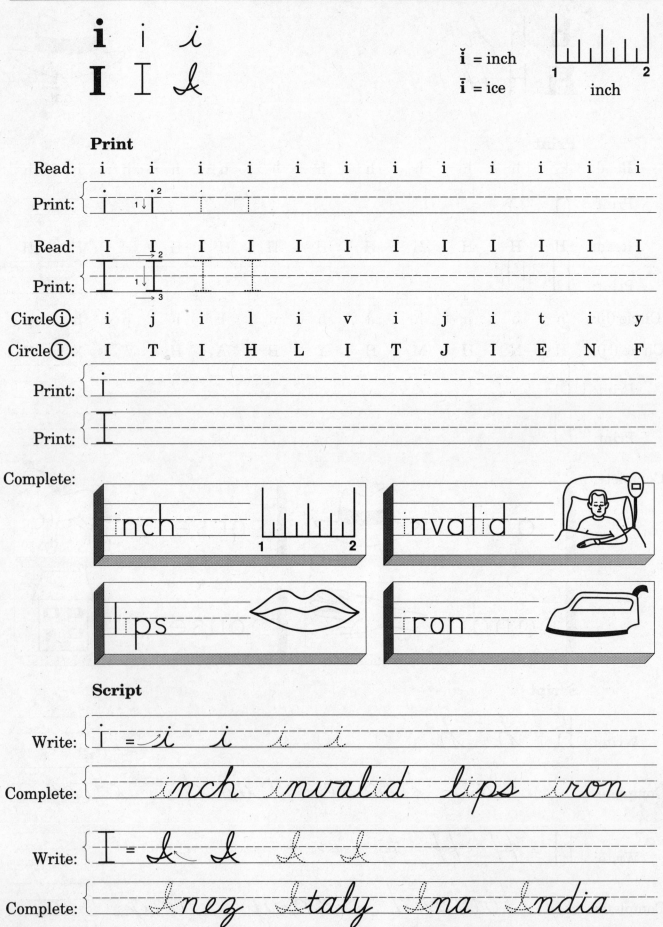

i i *i*

I I *I*

ĭ = inch
ī = ice

inch

Print

Read: i   i   i   i   i   i   i   i   i   i   i

Print:

Read: I   I   I   I   I   I   I   I   I   I   I

Print:

Circle ⓘ: i   j   i   l   i   v   i   j   i   t   i   y

Circle Ⓘ: I   T   I   H   L   I   T   J   I   E   N   F

Print: i

Print: I

Complete:

inch

invalid

lips

iron

Script

Write: i = *i   i   i   i*

Complete: *inch   invalid   lips   iron*

Write: I = *I   I   I   I*

Complete: *Inez   Italy   Ina   India*

j j *j*
J J *J*

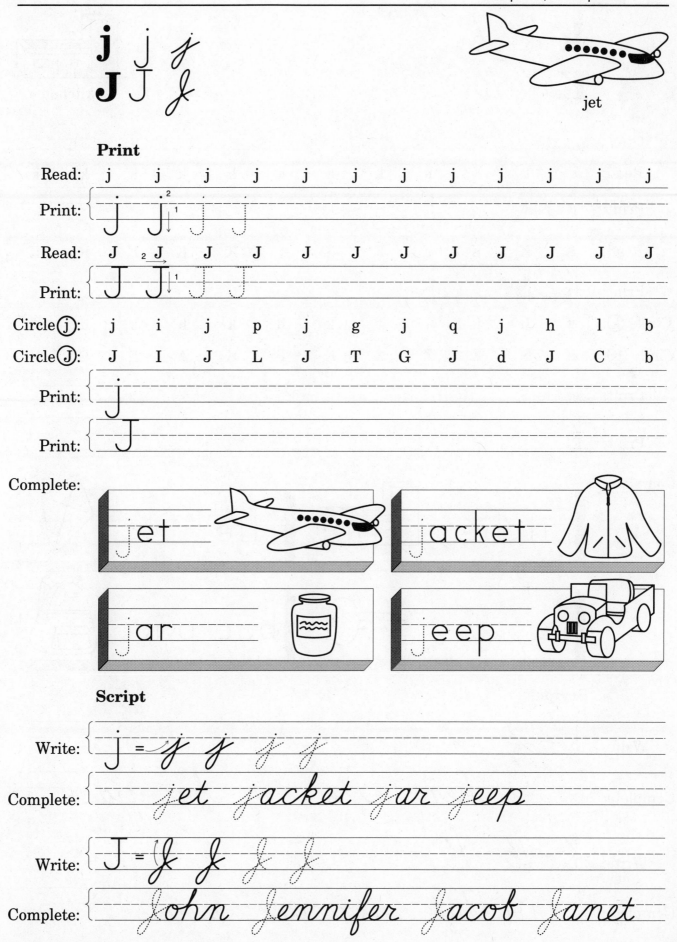

jet

Print

Read: j   j   j   j   j   j   j   j   j   j   j   j

Print: j   j   j   j

Read: J   J   J   J   J   J   J   J   J   J   J   J

Print: J   J   J   J

Circle ⓙ:   j   i   j   p   j   g   j   q   j   h   l   b

Circle Ⓙ:   J   I   J   L   J   T   G   J   d   J   C   b

Print: j

Print: J

Complete:

jet

jacket

jar

jeep

Script

Write: j = *j j j j*

Complete: *jet jacket jar jeep*

Write: J = *J J J J*

Complete: *John Jennifer Jacob Janet*

k k *k*

K K *K*

kitchen

Print

Read: k   k   k   k   k   k   k   k   k   k   k   k

Print: k   k   k   k

Read: K   K   K   K   K   K   K   K   K   K   K   K

Print: K   K   K   K

Circle ⓚ:   k   h   k   l   t   k   h   k   b   k   d   f

Circle Ⓚ:   K   N   K   Z   X   K   P   K   A   R   E   Y

Print: k

Print: K

Complete:

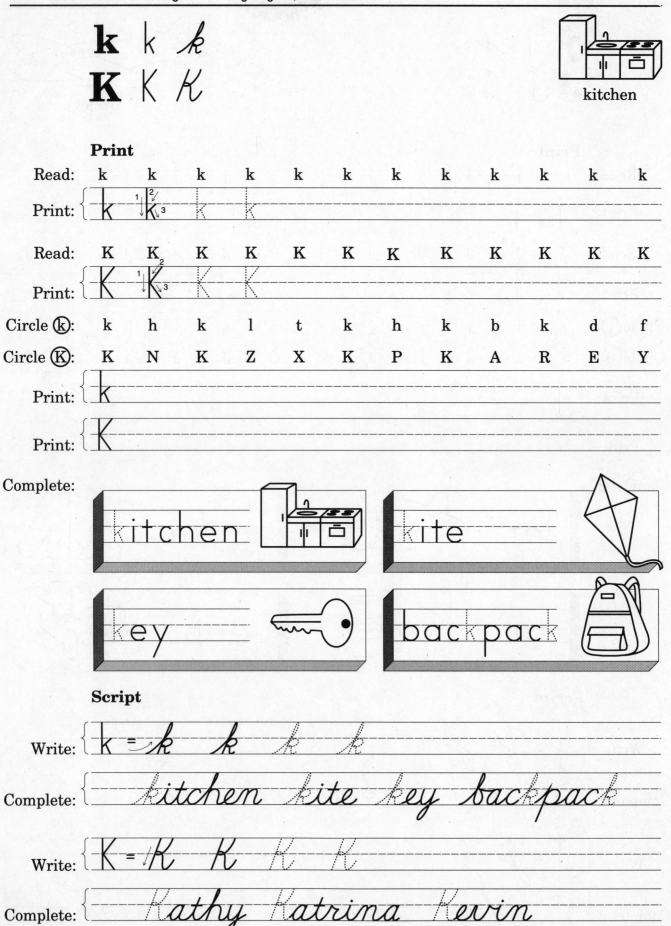

kitchen

kite

key

backpack

Script

Write: k = k   k   k   k

Complete: kitchen kite key backpack

Write: K = K   K   K   K

Complete: Kathy Katrina Kevin

l | l | l
L | L | L

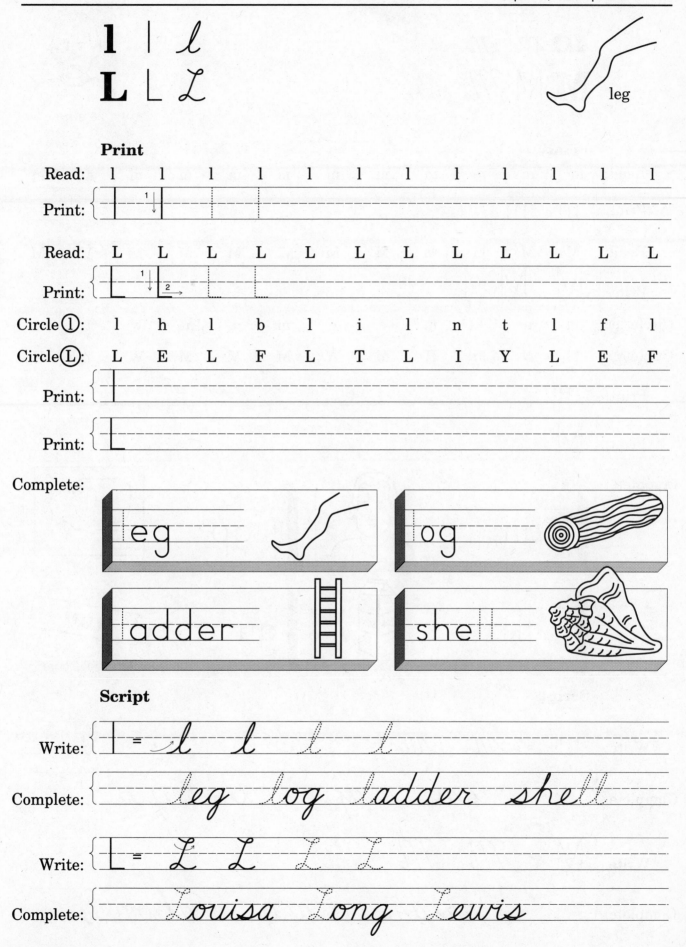

leg

Print

Read: l l l l l l l l l l l l

Print: {

Read: L L L L L L L L L L L L

Print: {

Circle ①: l h l b l i l n t l f l

Circle Ⓛ: L E L F L T L I Y L E F

Print: {

Print: {

Complete:

eg

og

adder

she

Script

Write: { l = l l l l

Complete: { leg log ladder shell

Write: { L = L L L L

Complete: { Louisa Long Lewis

m m _m_
M M _M_

man

Print

Read: m   m   m   m   m   m   m   m   m   m   m

Print: m   m   m   m

Read: M   M   M   M   M   M   M   M   M   M   M

Print: M   M   M   M

Circle m: m   n   h   m   z   e   m   i   u   w   m   v

Circle M: M   N   M   H   M   W   M   V   M   W   Z   Y

Print: m

Print: M

Complete:

man

map

milk

gum

Script

Write: m = _m_   _m_   _m_   _m_

Complete: _man   map   milk   gum_

Write: M = _M_   _M_   _M_   _M_

Complete: _Marian   Mary   Mahoney_

n n *n*

N N *N*

nut

Print

Read: n   n   n   n   n   n   n   n   n   n   n

Print: n   n   n   n

Read: N   N   N   N   N   N   N   N   N   N   N

Print: N   N   N   N

Circle (n): n   m   n   u   n   h   n   b   d   n   o   z

Circle (N): N   M   Z   N   H   N   F   E   N   W   V   Y

Print: n

Print: N

Complete:

nut

nurse

net

pan

Script

Write: n = *n   n   n   n*

Complete: *nut   nurse   net   pan*

Write: N = *N   N   N   N*

Complete: *Nancy   Nepal   Nevada*

o o *o*
O O *O*

ŏ = octopus

ō = ocean

octopus

Print

Read: o   o   o   o   o   o   o   o   o   o   o   o

Print: O   O   ⊙   ⊙

Read: O   O   O   O   O   O   O   O   O   O   O   O

Print: O   O   ⊙   ⊙

Circle (o):   o   c   o   u   o   p   o   q   e   r   o   a

Circle (O):   O   D   O   Q   O   C   U   O   Q   D   B   P

Print: O

Print: O

Complete:

octopus

sock

orange

boat

Script

Write: O = *O   O   O   O*

Complete: *octopus sock orange boat*

Write: O = *O   O   O   O*

Complete: *Oscar   Olivia   Orange*

p p p
P P P

pig

Print

Read: p   p   p   p   p   p   p   p   p   p   p   p

Print: P P P P

Read: P   P₂ P   P   P   P   P   P   P   P   P   P

Print: P P P P

Circle (p): p   d   p   b   p   q   p   g   p   q   p   j

Circle (P): P   B   D   Q   H   P   F   P   J   B   G   D

Print: p

Print: P

Complete:

pig

pan

pen

pup

Script

Write: p = p p p p

Complete: pig pan pen pup

Write: P = P P P P

Complete: Pam Peter Paula Pat

q q q
Q Q Q

quilt

Print

Read: q q q q q q q q q q q q

Print: q q q q

Read: Q Q Q Q Q Q Q Q Q Q Q Q

Print: Q Q Q Q

Circle q: q g q p q h q d q j q b

Circle Q: Q O D Q X Q Y Q D P Q C

Print: q

Print: Q

Complete:

quilt

quiet   "Sh!"

quarter

quart   1 QT.

Script

Write: q = q q q q

Complete: quilt quiet quarter quart

Write: Q = Q Q Q Q

Complete: Quaker Quebec Queen

r r r
R R R

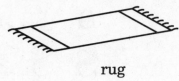

rug

Print

Read: r r r r r r r r r r r

Print: r r r r

Read: R R R R R R R R R R R

Print: R R R R

Circle ⓡ: r n r h r m r z o r u c

Circle Ⓡ: R P R B R D R T R P S R

Print: r

Print: R

Complete:

rug

ring

rat

car

Script

Write: r = r r r r

Complete: rug ring rat car

Write: R = R R R R

Complete: Richard Rachel Robert Ray

s s s

S S S

sun

Print

Read: s s s s s s s s s s s s

Print: S S S S

Read: S S S S S S S S S S S S

Print: S S S S

Circle ⓢ: s c s e s z s x n a s c

Circle Ⓢ: S B S R D S O P C S Z C

Print: S

Print: S

Complete:

sun

sneakers

spoon

stove

Script

Write: S = s s s s

Complete: sun sneakers spoon stove

Write: S = S S S S

Complete: Sanchez Stephen Salvador

t † *t*
T T *J*

television
(TV)

Print

Read: t   t   t   t   t   t   t   t   t   t   t   t   t

Print: †

Read: T   T   T   T   T   T   T   T   T   T   T   T   T

Print: T

Circle ⓣ:   t   l   t   i   j   k   t   y   h   t   l   i

Circle Ⓣ:   T   I   T   L   T   E   F   T   I   Z   H   J

Print: †

Print: T

Complete:

television

truck

telephone

tire

Script

Write: † = *t*   *t*   *t*   *t*

Complete: *television truck telephone tire*

Write: T = *J*   *J*   *J*   *J*

Complete: *Jim Theresa Tom Tony*

u u *u*
U U *U*

ŭ = umbrella
ū = tube

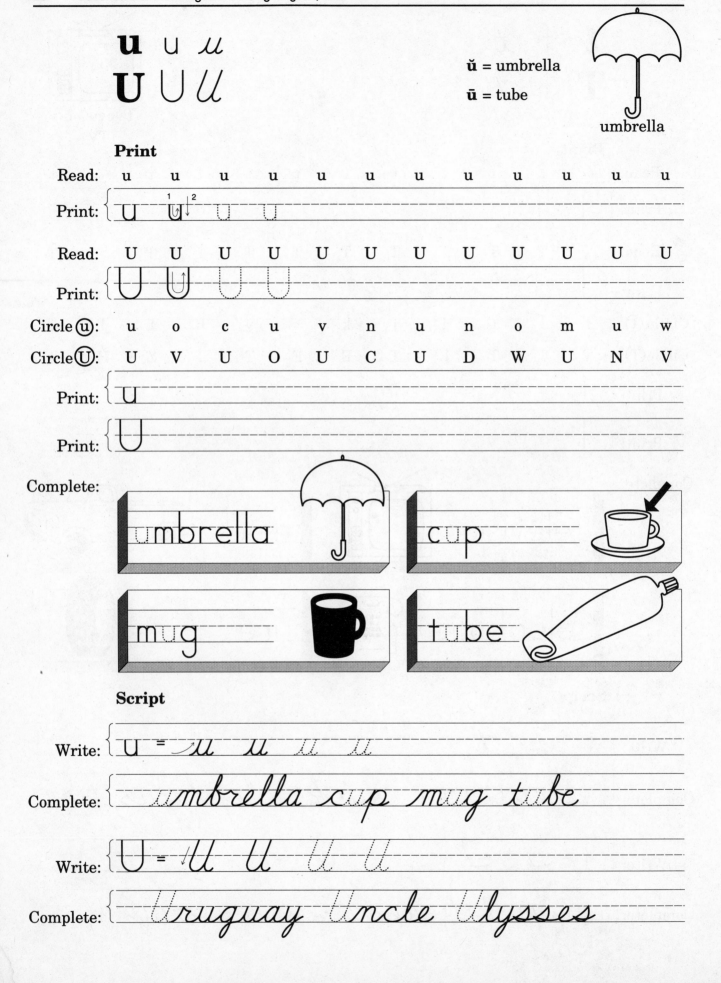

umbrella

Print

Read: u   u   u   u   u   u   u   u   u   u   u   u

Print:

Read: U   U   U   U   U   U   U   U   U   U   U   U

Print:

Circle ⓤ:   u   o   c   u   v   n   u   n   o   m   u   w

Circle Ⓤ:   U   V   U   O   U   C   U   D   W   U   N   V

Print: u

Print: U

Complete:

umbrella

cup

mug

tube

Script

Write: U = *u u u u*

Complete: *umbrella cup mug tube*

Write: U = *U U U U*

Complete: *Uruguay Uncle Ulysses*

v v *v*
V V *U*

van

Print

Read: v   v   v   v   v   v   v   v   v   v   v   v

Print: V   V₁₂   V   V

Read: V   V   V   V   V   V   V   V   V   V   V   V

Print: V   V₁₂   V   V

Circle (v): v   w   v   u   v   n   x   v   y   v   z   w

Circle (V): V   W   V   N   V   M   V   Y   Z   V   A   V

Print: V

Print: V

Complete:

van

vest

vacuum

vase

Script

Write: V = *v   v   v   v*

Complete: *van vest vacuum vase*

Write: V = *U   U   U   U*

Complete: *Virginia Venezuela Venice*

w w *w*
W *WW*

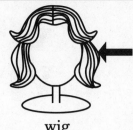

wig

Print

Read: w   w   w   w   w   w   w   w   w   w   w   w

Print: W   W   W   W

Read: W   W   W   W   W   W   W   W   W   W   W   W

Print: W   W   W   W

Circle ⓦ:   w   v   w   m   x   w   n   v   y   w   z   r

Circle Ⓦ:   W   V   W   M   W   N   W   X   W   Y   Z   H

Print: W

Print: W

Complete:

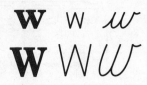

wig

wallet

washer

saw

Script

Write: W = *w*   *w*   *w*   *w*

Complete: *wig wallet washer saw*

Write: W = *W*   *W*   *W*   *W*

Complete: *Warsaw West Indies William*

x x _x_
X X _X_

x (ks) = box

x (z) = xylophone

box

Print

Read: x   x   x   x   x   x   x   x   x   x   x   x

Print: X   X   X   X

Read: X   X   X   X   X   X   X   X   X   X   X   X

Print: X   X   X   X

Circle ⓧ:   x   y   x   w   x   v   x   y   x   z   x   x

Circle Ⓧ:   X   Y   X   Z   X   W   N   X   V   A   K   M

Print: X

Print: X

Complete:

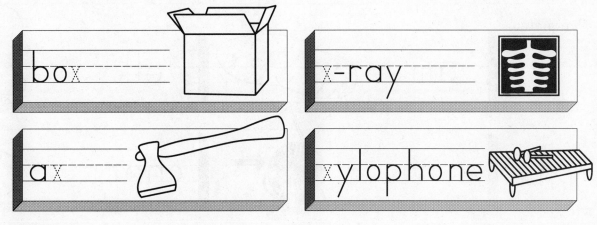

box

x-ray

ax

xylophone

Script

Write: X = _X_   _X_   _X_   _X_

Complete: _box x-ray ax xylophone_

Write: X = _X_   _X_   _X_   _X_

Complete: _Xerox Xavier Xingu_

y y *y*
Y Y *Y*

y = yam
y (ē) = baby
y (ī) = sky
y (ĭ) = syrup   yam

Print

Read: y   y   y   y   y   y   y   y   y   y   y   y

Print: Y Y Y Y

Read: Y   Y   Y   Y   Y   Y   Y   Y   Y   Y   Y   Y

Print: Y Y Y Y

Circle ⓨ:   y   v   y   j   g   y   p   y   q   v   y   x

Circle Ⓨ:   Y   V   K   W   Y   N   M   Y   W   X   Z   A

Print: Y

Print: Y

Complete:

yam

yell

yarn

cherry

Script

Write: Y = y y y y

Complete: yam yell yarn cherry

Write: Y = Y Y Y Y

Complete: Yalta Yellow River Yokohama

z z *z*
Z Z *Z*

zipper

Print

Read: z   z   z   z   z   z   z   z   z   z   z   z

Print: Z   Z   Z   Z

Read: Z   Z   Z   Z   Z   Z   Z   Z   Z   Z   Z   Z

Print: Z   Z   Z   Z

Circle ⓩ:   z   x   z   y   s   z   v   w   z   k   z   x

Circle Ⓩ:   Z   X   Z   Y   T   S   V   Z   W   M   Z   N

Print: Z

Print: Z

Complete:

zipper

zero   0 1 2 3 4 5

zucchini

zebra

Script

Write: Z = *z z z z*

Complete: *zipper zero zucchini zebra*

Write: Z = *Z Z Z Z*

Complete: *Zen Zagreb Zanzibar*

DOUBLE CONSONANTS

Two letters that are alike make one sound.

	Sounds			**Words**					
1. ll = l:	ll	ll	bell	tell	pill	bell	tell	pill
2. ss = s:	ss	ss	miss	less	Bess	miss	less	Bess
3. ff = f:	ff	ff	puff	cuff	Jeff	puff	cuff	Jeff
4. zz = z:	zz	zz	buzz	fuzz	fizz	buzz	fuzz	fizz

Write:

1. bell
2. tell
3. pill
4. miss
5. less
6. Bess
7. puff
8. cuff
9. Jeff
10. buzz
11. fuzz
12. fizz

Listen and write:

1.   4.

2.   5.

3.   6.

UNIT TWO:
Short-Vowel Words

In Chapters 3 through 11, you will read, write, and review one-syllable, three-letter words that use the five short vowels:

Short Vowel	Example
ĭ	dig
ă	sat
ŏ	job
ŭ	bus
ĕ	men

You will also learn related sight words.

CHAPTER 3:
Words with the ĭ Sound

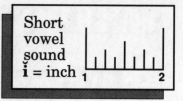

Short vowel sound
ĭ = inch

SOUNDS

Read: | bi | di | fi | gi | hi | ji | ki | li | mi | ni |

pi | qui | ri | si | ti | vi | wi | yi | zi

Write: {
_____
- - - - - - - - - - - - - - - - - - - -
_____

{
_____
- - - - - - - - - - - - - - - - - - - -
_____

Listen and write: {
_____
- - - - - - - - - - - - - - - - - - - -
_____

{
_____
- - - - - - - - - - - - - - - - - - - -
_____

SOUNDS AND WORDS

Read:

b	bi	bid	big	bill	Bill	bin	bit	
d	di	did	dig	dill	dim	din	dip	
f	fi	fib	fig	fill	fin	fit	fix	fizz
g	gi	gig	gill	Gil				
h	hi	hid	hill	him	hip	his	hit	
j	ji	jib	jig	Jill	Jim			
k	ki	kid	kill	Kim	kin	kiss	kit	Kit
l	li	lid	Lil	Lin	lip	lit		
m	mi	mid	mill	miss	Miss	mitt	mix	
n	ni	nib	nil	nip	nix			
p	pi	pig	pill	pin	pip	pit		
qu	qui	quid	quill	quip	quit	quiz		
r	ri	rib	rid	rig	rill	rim	rip	
s	si	Sid	sill	sin	sip	sit	six	
t	ti	till	Tim	tin	tip			
v	vi	vim	Vin	Viv				
w	wi	wig	will	Will	win	wit	wiz	
y	yi	yip						
z	zi	zig	zip					
	i	if	it	is	in	ill	inn	

Sight Words

give {

live {

The e is silent. Ignore it. Pronounce these sight words like the words on the chart.

qu {

The letter u always follows the letter q.

The, the

WORDS

Read
and
write: big

pig

bit

pill

six

dig

did

win

mix

it

will

quit

live

in

his

rig

Miss

Kim

give

fig

tin

bin

Jim

hid

Listen
and
write: 1.

7.

2.

8.

3.

9.

4.

10.

5.

11.

6.

12.

READ, CIRCLE, WRITE

Read: Circle the correct picture: Write:

1. big pig

2. bit pill

3. six dig

4. mix it

5. live in

6. zip it

7. Jim hid

8. give fig

SPECIAL SOUNDS: th, Th

These two letters make one new sound—**th.**
Use your throat to pronounce **th**, as in **the.**

Read: th   Th   th   Th   th   th   th   th   Th   th   th   th

Write: {
_____
_____

Listen
and {
_____
write:
_____

Compare

Read: t   t   t   T   t   t   H   h   h   h   h   h

th   Th   th   th   th   t   h   Th   t   h   th   t   h   th

Write: {
_____
_____

Listen
and {
_____
write:
_____

Words

Read: Write: Read: Write:

1. the, The   {_____   4. this, This   {_____
              _____   _____

2. then, Then {_____   5. than, Than   {_____
              _____   _____

3. them, Them {_____   6. that, That   {_____
              _____   _____

NOTE: Sometimes **th** is pronounced without the throat, using the teeth and tongue only.

Read: Write: Read: Write:

1. with {_____   3. With {_____
         _____   _____

2. thin {_____   4. Thin {_____
         _____   _____

Listen and write:

1. {_____   2. {_____   3. {_____   4. {_____
   _____   _____   _____   _____

SIGHT WORD: the, The

Read: the   the   the   the   The   The   The   The

Write:{ --

Read: Write:

1. the pig   { -------------------------------   { -------------------------------
                  -------------------------------   -------------------------------

2. the pill   { -------------------------------   { -------------------------------
                  -------------------------------   -------------------------------

3. the fig   { -------------------------------   { -------------------------------
                  -------------------------------   -------------------------------

4. Jim hid the pig.   { --
                        ----

5. Tim bit the fig.   { --
                        ----

6. Give Lin the pill. { --
                        ----

7. The lip   { -------------------------------   { -------------------------------
                   -------------------------------   -------------------------------

8. The mill   { -------------------------------   { -------------------------------
                   -------------------------------   -------------------------------

9. The bin   { -------------------------------   { -------------------------------
                   -------------------------------   -------------------------------

10. The lip is big.   { --
                        ----

11. The mill is lit. { --
                        ----

12. The bin is tin.   { --

Listen
and
write: 1.{ -----------------------------   4.{ -----------------------------
             -----------------------------   -----------------------------

         2.{ -----------------------------   5.{ -----------------------------
             -----------------------------   -----------------------------

         3.{ -----------------------------   6.{ -----------------------------
             -----------------------------   -----------------------------

         7.{ -----------------------------

SENTENCES: STATEMENTS

Read: Write:

1. The pig is big.

2. Bill bit the pill.

3. Six will dig the pit.

4. Jill will mix it.

5. Vin did live in the mill.

6. Viv will zip it.

7. Jim hid in this bin.

8. Kim did give him a fig.

9. The mill is big.

10. The pig did the jig.

11. Tim hid his mitt.

12. The fig is in the tin.

Listen and write:

1.

2.

3.

4.

5.

6.

Read: Write:

  1. Miss Kim hid the pin.

  2. Sid is ill.

  3. Jill will kiss Sid.

  4. The wig will fit.

  5. Tim hit his hip.

  6. The thin kid will quit.

  7. Bill did win.

  8. Give him the tip.

  9. The rig will tip.

 10. Fill the tin with it.

 11. Fix the mill.

 12. Jim did sip it.

Listen and write:

  1.

  2.

  3.

  4.

  5.

  6.

SENTENCES: QUESTIONS

These questions use the words **did, will,** and **is.**

Read: Write:

1. Did Tim bill him?

2. Did Jim dig in it?

3. Did the rig tip?

4. Did Kim miss Bill?

5. Did Tim mix the dip?

6. Did the pig nip him?

7. Did Jill win?

8. Did Lil fix the rig?

9. Will Bill quiz him?

10. Will Kim sit in it?

11. Will Viv fill the pit?

12. Will it tip him?

Listen and write:

1.

2.

3.

4.

5.

6.

Read: Write:

1. Will Vin hit with it?

2. Will the mitt fit him?

3. Will Jill rip it?

4. Will Tim dig in the hill?

5. Is it in it?

6. Is his pig big?

7. Is Tim in the mill?

8. Is Kim his kid?

9. Is the bin tin?

10. Is this mitt his?

11. Is Jill six?

12. Is the kit his?

Listen and write:

1.

2.

3.

4.

5.

6.

STORY

Read: **In the Mill**

The mill is big. Will Jim live in this mill? Will his kid, Kim, live in it? Jim will live in the mill if Kim will. Kim will live in it. Jim will live in the mill with Kim.

Jim will fix the mill. Kim, his kid, is big. Kim will fix the rig. Jim will fill the bin.

Jim will give Kim the pig. The pig will live in the mill. The pig will dig in the hill. The pig hid. Will the pig yip? Will Kim miss the pig?

Jim hit his hip in the mill. Jim is ill. Will Kim give him the pill? The pill is in the tin. Kim will give Jim the pill. The pill is big. Jim bit it. Jim bit his lip. Jim will sit in the mill with Kim. Will Jim quit the mill?

Write:

_____

_____

_____

_____

_____

_____

_____

_____

_____

_____

_____

BONUS PAGE

Read statements:

1. If Tim is ill, Bill will give him the pill.

2. Jill will live in the mill if it is big.

Write:

1. {
_____
_____
{
_____
_____

2. {
_____
_____
{
_____
_____

Listen and write:

{
_____
_____

{
_____
_____

Read questions:

1. If Tim is ill, will Bill give him the pill?

2. Will Jill live in the mill if it is big?

Write:

1. {
_____
_____
{
_____
_____

2. {
_____
_____
{
_____
_____

Listen and write:

{
_____
_____

{
_____
_____

CHAPTER 4:
Words with the ă Sound

SOUNDS

Read: ba   ca   da   fa   ga   ha   la   ma

na   pa   ra   sa   ta   va   ya   za

Write: { _____

_____

Listen
and { _____
write:
_____

{ _____

_____

SOUNDS AND WORDS

Sight Words

Read:

b	ba	bad	bag	ban	bat			
c	ca	cab	cad	can	cap	cat		
d	da	dab	dad	Dad	dam	Dan		
f	fa	fad	fan	fat				
g	ga	gab	gad	gag	gal	gap	gas	
h	ha	had	hag	ham	has	hat		
j	ja	jab	jag	jam	Jan			
l	la	lab	lad	lag	lap	lass		
m	ma	mad	man	map	mass	mat	Matt	Max
n	na	nab	nag	Nan	nap			
p	pa	pad	pal	Pam	pan	pass	pat	Pat
r	ra	rag	ram	ran	rap	rat		
s	sa	sad	sag	Sal	Sam	sap	sass	sat
t	ta	tab	tag	tam	tan	tap	tax	
v	va	Val	van	Van	vat			
y	ya	yak	yam	yap	Yap	Yan		
z	za	zag	zap					
	a	ad	add	am	Ann	and	as	at	ax

have { The **e** is silent. Ignore it. Pronounce this sight word like the words on the chart.

I, you, they
we, he, she, be
are
A, a

WORDS

Read
and
write: fat {

cat {

Pam {

sat {

has {

bag {

dad {

hat {

mad {

man {

sad {

pal {

tag {

tax {

cab {

gas {

jam {

can {

rag {

mat {

ham {

pan {

ram {

van {

Listen
and
write: 1. {

7. {

2. {

8. {

3. {

9. {

4. {

10. {

5. {

11. {

6. {

12. {

READ, CIRCLE, WRITE

Read: Circle the correct picture: Write:

1. fat cat

2. Pam sat

3. has bag

4. dad hat

5. mad man

6. sad pal

7. tag tax $1.00 $1.00
                              .05 tax
                              $1.05

8. cab gas   CAB   CAB

SENTENCES

Read: Write:

1. The cat is fat.

2. Pam sat in it.

3. Nan has the bag.

4. His dad has the hat.

5. The man is mad.

6. His pal is sad.

7. The tag has the tax.

8. The cab has gas.

Listen and write:

1.

2.

3.

4.

5.

6.

7.

8.

SIGHT WORD: a, A

The word **a** means "one."   The word **a** sounds different from **ă**.
The word **a** rhymes with **the.**   (Say **a =uh.**)

Read: a   a   a   a   A   A   A   A

Write: {

Read: Write:

1. a bag   {

2. a hat   {

3. a map   {

4. Nan has a bag. {

5. Max has a hat. {

6. Sam has a map. {

7. A man   {

8. A van   {

9. A cab   {

10. A man sat. {

11. A van is tan. {

12. A cab has gas. {

Listen
and   1. {   4. {
write:

         2. {   5. {

         3. {   6. {

SPECIAL SKILL: Comparing **a** and **an**

A or **a** is used before words that begin with consonant sounds.

> **Examples:** **A** cat is big. It is **a** big cat.

An or **an** means the same as **a** but is used before words that begin with vowel sounds.

> **Examples:** **An** inch is not big. It is **an** inch long.

Consonant Sounds

Read: Write:

1. a bag {

2. a cat {

3. a hat {

4. a man {

5. a pill {

6. a can {

7. a rat {

8. a fig {

9. a tax {

Vowel Sounds

Read: Write:

10. an ăx {

11. an ĕgg {

12. an ĭnch {

13. an ŏctopus {

14. an ŭmbrella {

15. an āpe {

16. an ēagle {

17. an īcicle {

18. an ōcean {

Special Cases

+ The vowel **u** sometimes sounds hard like a consonant **y.**

* The consonant **h** is sometimes silent, so words begin with the first vowel sound.

Read: Write:

+ 1. a yam {

+ 2. a union {

Read: Write:

* 3. an herb {

* 4. an heir {

Listen and write:

1. {

2. {

3. {

4. {

5. {

6. {

7. {

8. {

9. {

10. {

11. {

12. {

13. {

14. {

15. {

16. {

17. {

18. {

Write **a** or **an**:

1. {   mill

2. {   wig

3. {   rat

4. {   ring

5. {   bin

6. {   ax

7. {   inn

8. {   umbrella

9. {   inch

10. {   ham

11. {   herb

12. {   union

SPECIAL SKILL: PLURALS

Final **s** means "more than one."

one cat      two cats      six cats

1   2   6

Read:

Singular (one)	Plural (more than one)
1. cat	cats
2. rat	rats
3. pig	pigs
4. wig	wigs
5. van	vans
6. cab	cabs

Write:

Singular (one)	Plural (more than one)
{ _____	{ _____
{ _____	{ _____
{ _____	{ _____
{ _____	{ _____
{ _____	{ _____
{ _____	{ _____

Read and write plural sentences:

1. Bill has six cats.   { _____

2. Jan has six wigs.   { _____

Listen and write:

Singular (one)	Plural (more than one)
1. { _____	{ _____
2. { _____	{ _____
3. { _____	{ _____
4. { _____	{ _____

SPECIAL SKILL: Comparing **has** and **have**

Read and write:

1. Nan has a cab.

{_____

2. Vin has a cab.

{_____

3. Nan and Vin have cabs.

{_____

4. Dan and Sam have a van.

{_____

5. Jill and Dan have a mill.

{_____

6. Jill and Pam have a cab.

{_____

SPECIAL SKILL: The verb **to be** (present tense)

Sight Words

Singular	Plural
I am	we are
you are*	you are*
he is	
she is	they are
it is**	

*__You are__ is used for singular "you" as well as plural "you."

Use **it with nonhuman things.

Read and write:

1. to be

2. I am

3. he is

4. she is

5. it is

6. we are

7. you are

8. they are

Listen and write:

1.

2.

3.

4.

5.

6.

7.

8.

Complete with a form of **to be.**

1. to
2. I
3. he
4. she
5. it
6. we
7. you
8. they

1. _____ be
2. _____ am
3. _____ is
4. _____ is
5. _____ is
6. _____ are
7. _____ are
8. _____ are

Complete with a form of **to be.**

1. I _____ on a bus.
2. He _____ a man.
3. She _____ a mom.
4. It _____ a dog.

5. We _____ at the mill.
6. You _____ in the cab.
7. They _____ cats.
8. They _____ tots.

Listen and write:

1.
2.
3.
4.

5.
6.
7.
8.

SENTENCES: STATEMENTS

Read: Write:

1. The cat sat.

2. Sam has an ax.

3. The cab has gas.

4. Dan can add.

5. Sam and his pal nap.

6. Jan has had a nap.

7. A rat ran.

8. A map is in that van.

9. The ham is in this bag.

10. The tag has a tax.

11. She has it in a can.

12. We are pals.

Listen and write:

1.

2.

3.

4.

5.

6.

Read: Write:

1. It is an ant.

2. You are as fat as I am!

3. Dan is in an ad.

4. Dad has to be at the mill.

5. I am at bat.

6. Sid and Pam have had a quiz.

7. Bill and Jim have six cats.

8. He and I have a cat.

9. Nan and Jan have six wigs.

10. They have a wig.

11. Bill and Nan have six bags.

12. They are tan bags.

Listen and write:

1.

2.

3.

4.

5.

6.

7.

SENTENCES: QUESTIONS

These questions use the words **did, will, is, can, have, has, are,** and **am.**

Read: Write:

1. Will Nan sit?

2. Did Sal pat the cats?

3. Is that a tan hat?

4. Can Sam tag Jan?

5. Have Tim and Val quit?

6. Will Pam pass Dan?

7. Did the cab have gas?

8. Am I fat?

9. Can Max fill the bags?

10. Have the kids sat in the van?

11. Will the van have a tax?

12. Did the kid have a nap?

Listen and write:

1.

2.

3.

4.

5.

6.

Read: Write:

1. Is she sad?

2. Can Van add six and six?

3. Has Pat had a yam?

4. Will Ann bat and hit?

5. Did the man have an ax?

6. Is the jam in this can?

7. Can the man tax the fans?

8. Are they in the cab?

9. Will Miss Yap give a quiz?

10. Are you at the inn?

11. Are we in the mill?

12. Can the pals have cats?

Listen and write:

1.

2.

3.

4.

5.

6.

7.

STORY

Read: **The Tan Hats**

    Nan has a hat. The hat is tan. Sam has a hat. His hat is tan. Sam and Nan have tan hats. The hats have tags with the tax.

    The hats are in big bags. Are the bags in the van? Are they in the cab? Nan has a van. The bags with the hats are in the van.

    A fat cat sat in the van. Did the cat have a nap? The cat had a nap in the hat bags!

    The tan hats had big rips. The hats sag. Nan is sad. Sam is mad at that cat!

    The fat cat ran and ran. Sam and Nan will fix the rips in the tan hats.

Write:

BONUS PAGE

Read statements:

1. If the van has gas, it can pass the cab.

2. The hat will have a tax if it has a tan tag.

Write:

1.

2.

Listen and write:

Read questions:

1. If the van has gas, can it pass the cab?

2. Will the hat have a tax if it has a tan tag?

Write:

1.

2.

Listen and write:

CHAPTER 5:
Review of the ă and ĭ Sounds

SOUNDS

Read: Write:

   ă   ĭ   ă   ĭ

1. ba   bi

2. ca   -

3. da   di

4. fa   fi

5. ga   gi

6. ha   hi

7. ja   ji

8. -   ki

9. la   li

10. ma   mi

11. na   ni

12. pa   pi

13. -   qui

14. ra   ri

15. sa   si

16. ta   ti

17. va   vi   {——————————   {——————————

18. -   wi   {——————————   {——————————

19. ya   yi   {——————————   {——————————

20. za   zi   {——————————   {——————————

Listen and write (fixed order):

ă   ĭ

1. {——————————   {——————————

2. {——————————   {——————————

3. {——————————   {——————————

4. {——————————   {——————————

5. {——————————   {——————————

6. {——————————   {——————————

7. {——————————   {——————————

8. {——————————   {——————————

9. {——————————   {——————————

10. {——————————   {——————————

Listen and write (mixed order):

1. {——————————   {——————————

2. {——————————   {——————————

3. {——————————   {——————————

SOUND WORDS

Read: Write:

ă	ĭ		ă	ĭ

#	ă	ĭ
1.	bad	bid
2.	cab	-
3.	dam	dim
4.	fan	fin
5.	gal	gill
6.	has	his
7.	jam	Jim
8.	-	kid
9.	lap	lip
10.	mass	miss
11.	nab	nib
12.	pan	pin
13.	-	quill
14.	rag	rig
15.	sat	sit
16.	tan	tin
17.	van	Vin

18. -   win

19. yap   yip

20. zap   zip

Listen and write (fixed order):

ă   ĭ

1.

2.

3.

4.

5.

6.

7.

8.

9.

10.

Listen and write (mixed order):

1.

2.

3.

4.

SIGHT WORDS

Read: Write:

1. the   The

2. a   A

3. have   Have

4. give   Give

5. live   Live

6. are   Are

7. I   I

8. they   They

9. he   He

10. she   She

11. we   We

12. you   You

13. be   Be

Listen and write:

1.   4.   7.   10.

2.   5.   8.   11.

3.   6.   9.   12.

SENTENCES: STATEMENTS

Read and write:

1. The man ran with his kid.

2. Tim can sit in the cab with you.

3. That wig and this hat fit Nan.

4. A big ham is in the bag.

5. The mad cat bit the big rat.

6. That kid has a mitt, and I have a cap.

7. Bill can hit, and she can pass.

8. They are in a big jam and are mad.

9. If Jim and Dan live in the mill, they will miss Jill.

10. Sid will win if his van can pass the six big hills.

11. If Val and Pam dig the pit, we will fill it in.

12. Lin can pass the quiz if he can add.

SENTENCES: QUESTIONS

Read and write:

1. Will Pam sit with him?

2. Did Dan and Jill kiss?

3. Is Jan at the mill with you?

4. Can the cab pass that man?

5. Has he had a pill?

6. If the cab has gas, will it pass the van?

7. Will Sam dig the pit, and will Dan fill it?

8. Did the rat nip that kid?

9. Is the yam in this pan?

10. Can Sid and she have the map?

11. Are they pals with the big kids?

12. If Jim and I nag Dad, can we have the van?

Listen and write:

1. {

2. {

3. {

4. {

5. {

6. {

7. {

8. {

9. {

10. {

11. {

12. {

13. {

14. {

15. {

16. {

17. {

18. {

STORY

Read: **The Cab and the Big Van**

Dan has a big van. He can live in it. This van has a mat and six tin pans in it. In the van, Dan has a map with pins in it.

Dan has a pal. His pal is Bill. Bill has a tan cab.

Dan sat in his van. Bill sat in his cab. Dan, the man in the van, has a hat. Bill, the man in the cab, has a cap that fits him.

The van and the cab have gas. Dan ran the van, and Bill ran the cab. The hill is big! Can the big van pass the tan cab? Will Dan win? Will the cab ram the van? Will Bill win? Dan will fix his van if it is hit. Bill will fix his cab if it is hit. Will Bill quit? Will Dan quit?

The cab ran and ran. Bill did pass his pal in the big van! Bill, in the cab, did win! Dan, in the big van, is mad! Dan sat on his hat and bit his lip.

Write:

CHAPTER 6:
Words with the ŏ Sound

Short
vowel
sound
ŏ = octopus

SOUNDS

Read: bo   co   do   fo   go   ho   jo   lo   mo

           no   po   ro   so   to   vo   yo   zo

Write: {

Listen
and
write: {

SOUNDS AND WORDS

Read:

b	bo	bob	Bob	bog	bop	boss	box	
c	co	cob	cod	cog	con	cop	cot	
d	do	dog	doll	Don	dot	Dot		
f	fo	fog	fox					
g	go	gob	got					
h	ho	hog	hop	hot				
j	jo	job	jog	Jon	jot			
l	lo	lob	log	Lon	lop	loss	lot	
m	mo	mob	mod	mom	Mom	mop	moss	
n	no	nod	non	not				
p	po	pod	pop	Pop	pot	pox		
r	ro	rob	Rob	rod	Rod	Ron	rot	Roz
s	so	sob	sod	sop	sot			
t	to	Todd	Tom	top	toss	tot		
v	vo	Von						
y	yo	yon						
z	zo							
	o	off	on					

Sight Words

do

go

no

so

to

WORDS

Read
and
write: fox {

box {

not {

pot {

log {

rot {

mom {

mop {

tot {

sob {

pop {

boss {

got {

doll {

hog {

bog {

job {

cop {

hot {

dog {

fog {

cod {

cot {

mob {

Listen
and
write: 1. {

7. {

2. {

8. {

3. {

9. {

4. {

10. {

5. {

11. {

6. {

12. {

READ, CIRCLE, WRITE

Read: Circle the correct picture: Write:

1. fox box

2. not pot

3. log rot

4. mom job

5. pop toss

6. got doll

7. hog bog

8. cop cap

SENTENCES

Read: Write:

1. The fox is in the box.   _____

2. It is not a pot.   _____

3. The log did rot.   _____

4. His mom has a job.   _____

5. Pop can toss.   _____

6. Nan got a doll.   _____

7. The hog is in the bog.   _____

8. The cop has a cap.   _____

Listen and write:

1. _____

2. _____

3. _____

4. _____

5. _____

6. _____

7. _____

8. _____

SIGHT WORD: to, To

Read: to   to   to   to   To   To   To   To

Write: _____

Read statements: Write statements:

1. Dan ran to the mill.

2. Jim hit it to Kim.

3. Fill the can to the rim.

4. Vin ran to the cab.

5. Dan has to dig.

6. Dan and Jim have to jog.

7. Nan has to mop.

8. Nan and Dan have to fix it.

Read questions: Write questions:

1. Can Don hop to the log?

2. Did Jill have to jog?

Listen and write:

1.

2.

3.

4.

SIGHT WORD: do, Do

Read: do   do   do   do   Do   Do   Do   Do

Write: _____
         _____

Read statements: Write statements:

1. Jon will do it.   _____
                          _____

2. Ron and Tom do mop.   _____
                          _____

3. Roz can do the job.   _____
                          _____

4. Bob did do it.   _____
                          _____

5. Don had to do it.   _____
                          _____

Listen and write:

1. _____   2. _____
   _____   _____

Read questions: Write questions:

1. Do Roz and Todd jog?   _____
                          _____

2. Did Tom do the job?   _____
                          _____

3. Will Ron do it?   _____
                          _____

4. Is Bob the man to do it? _____
                          _____

5. Can Roz do it?   _____
                          _____

Listen and write:

1. _____
   _____

2. _____
   _____

SENTENCES: STATEMENTS

Read: Write:

  1. This pot is hot!

  2. No, the top is not hot.

  3. She has a job as a cop.

  4. Rip off that tag.

  5. The dog got off the cot.

  6. The doll is in an ad.

  7. An ax is on the logs.

  8. The fox ran to the bog.

  9. The hot dog is in the box.

10. They have to jog till we go.

11. Todd and I will do the job.

12. The cop got the hot rod.

Listen and write:

1.

2.

3.

4.

5.

6.

Read: Write:

  1. They are not in a big box.

  2. No, Von did not have it.

  3. Don has to nod to his boss.

  4. On his job, he has to mop.

  5. You are not to hit the dog!

  6. Toss the mop on top of it.

  7. Dad will mop so Mom can go.

  8. Dot has got to go to the inn.

  9. Roz and Tom have got to do it.

  10. Bob and I do not have to do it.

  11. We are off to do the job.

  12. I am at a loss!

Listen and write:

  1.

  2.

  3.

  4.

  5.

  6.

  7.

SENTENCES: QUESTIONS

These questions use the words **did, will, is, can, have, has, are, am,** and **do**.

Read: Write:

1. Did Bob box?

2. Will the dog hop off the cot?

3. Is Don in that mob?

4. Is the ax on a log?

5. Have Rob and Roz had naps?

6. Has Todd fit the rig?

7. Do Jon and Lon have to mop?

8. Is the job in an ad?

9. Are we to do this job?

10. Is the top hot?

11. Can Roz and I give it a toss?

12. Are they with Bob and Don?

Listen and write:

1.

2.

3.

4.

5.

6.

Read: Write:

1. Am I as big as Tom?

2. Are you and Dot on that job?

3. Did his mom have a mop?

4. Will the fox fit in the box?

5. Is the log in the bog?

6. Can the doll have a wig?

7. Have Ron and he got rods?

8. Has Roz got a boss?

9. Do the fox and the dog nip?

10. Did the cop nod to Bob?

11. Will the pot have a top?

12. Do Lon and she do the bop?

Listen and write:

1.

2.

3.

4.

5.

6.

7.

STORY

Read: **Roz and the Doll**

Roz is a tot. She has a doll. The doll is Dot. This doll is in a box. The box is on the cot.

Roz has a dog. The dog is Tom. Tom is a big dog.

Tom got on the cot. The big dog got the box with the doll. Tom got the top off the box. He got Dot, the doll. Roz got mad. "No, Tom, no!" Bad Tom hit the doll! Big, bad Tom bit the doll!

Roz got sad. Roz did sob and sob. Mom got mad at the dog. "Go, Tom!" So the dog did go. Tom ran to the hill. Big, bad Tom hid in a log. Tom, the big dog, is sad. He is not so bad.

Can Roz fix Dot, the doll? No. Mom did kiss Roz. "Do not sob, Roz. I can fix the doll, and I will do that."

Write:

BONUS PAGE

Read statements:

1. If Dot is a cop, she will have a cap, a van, a dog, and a boss.

2. Jon will not box if Bob and Don do not jog.

Write:

1. {_____

2. {_____

Listen and write:

{_____

Read questions:

1. If the hill is not big, can Roz hop to the top?

2. Will the doll have a tag if it is in a box?

Write:

1. {_____

2. {_____

Listen and write:

{_____

CHAPTER 7:
Review of the ă, ĭ, and ŏ Sounds

SOUNDS

Read: Write:

ă	ĭ	ŏ	ă	ĭ	ŏ
1. ba	bi	bo			
2. ca	-	co			
3. da	di	do			
4. fa	fi	fo			
5. ga	gi	go			
6. ha	hi	ho			
7. ja	ji	jo			
8. -	ki	-			
9. la	li	lo			
10. ma	mi	mo			
11. na	ni	no			
12. pa	pi	po			
13. -	qui	-			
14. ra	ri	ro			
15. sa	si	so			
16. ta	ti	to			

17. va   vi   vo

18. -   wi   -

19. ya   yi   yo

20. za   zi   zo

Listen and write (fixed order):

ă	ĭ	ŏ
1.		
2.		
3.		
4.		
5.		
6.		
7.		
8.		
9.		
10.		

Listen and write (mixed order):

1.		
2.		
3.		
4.		

SOUND WORDS

Read: Write:

ă	ĭ	ŏ		ă		ĭ		ŏ

1. bad   bid   Bob

2. cab   -   cop

3. dam   dig   doll

4. fan   fit   fox

5. gal   gill   got

6. has   hip   hot

7. jam   jib   jog

8. -   kid   -

9. lap   lip   log

10. man   miss   mop

11. nag   nib   not

12. pan   pill   pot

13. -   quill -

14. ran   rip   rob

15. sag   sin   sob

16. tax   tin   top

17. van   vim   Von

18. -   win   -

19. yam   yip   yon   { _____   { _____   { _____

20. zap   zig   -   { _____   { _____   { _____

Listen and write (fixed order):

	ă	ĭ	ŏ
1.	{ _____	{ _____	{ _____
2.	{ _____	{ _____	{ _____
3.	{ _____	{ _____	{ _____
4.	{ _____	{ _____	{ _____
5.	{ _____	{ _____	{ _____
6.	{ _____	{ _____	{ _____
7.	{ _____	{ _____	{ _____
8.	{ _____	{ _____	{ _____
9.	{ _____	{ _____	{ _____
10.	{ _____	{ _____	{ _____

Listen and write (mixed order):

1.	{ _____	{ _____	{ _____
2.	{ _____	{ _____	{ _____
3.	{ _____	{ _____	{ _____
4.	{ _____	{ _____	{ _____
5.	{ _____	{ _____	{ _____

SIGHT WORDS

Read: Write: Read: Write:

1. the   The {_____   10. so   So   {_____
                _____   _____

2. a   A   {_____   11. I   I   {_____
                _____   _____

3. have   Have {_____   12. are   Are {_____
                _____   _____

4. give   Give {_____   13. you   You {_____
                _____   _____

5. live   Live {_____   14. they They {_____
                _____   _____

6. to   To   {_____   15. we   We   {_____
                _____   _____

7. do   Do   {_____   16. he   He   {_____
                _____   _____

8. no   No   {_____   17. she   She {_____
                _____   _____

9. go   Go   {_____   18. be   Be   {_____
                _____   _____

Listen and write:

1. {_____ {_____ {_____ {_____

2. {_____ {_____ {_____ {_____

3. {_____ {_____ {_____ {_____

4. {_____ {_____ {_____ {_____

5. {_____ {_____ {_____ {_____

6. {_____ {_____ {_____ {_____

7. {_____ {_____ {_____ {_____

8. {_____ {_____ {_____ {_____

9. {_____ {_____ {_____ {_____

SENTENCES: STATEMENTS

Read and write:

1. The doll fit in a big box.

2. You are not to sit on this mat!

3. We got the bad dog that bit his hog.

4. The job in the lab is in an ad.

5. Jan and he got jobs at an inn.

6. Tom will have a nap on this cot.

7. Do not hit the cat!

8. Max and I will live in his van.

9. Give the doll to the kid so she can have it.

10. Yan and Kim have to do it, and they are mad.

11. If moss is on the logs, Nan got the logs in the bog.

12. If Jon can mop the van, his mom and dad will not have to do it.

SENTENCES: QUESTIONS

Read and write:

1. Did Dad quit his job at the mill?

2. Will the boss give the tip to Van?

3. Is this cat as big as that dog?

4. Can Lon have the mop and the pot?

5. Do the kids nap on the cot?

6. Has she got a lot to dig on the hill?

7. Did Miss Kim and the boss add a tag and the tax?

8. Are the six dogs in the box?

9. Can he fit the fat hog and the big pig in his van?

10. Are we to give the pots and pans to the man at the mill?

11. If the mat is in the van, will you give it to Bob?

12. Will Jan and Von win if they are at bat and hit?

Listen and write:

1. {

2. {

3. {

4. {

5. {

6. {

7. {

8. {

9. {

10. {

11. {

12. {

13. {

14. {

15. {

16. {

17. {

18. {

STORY

Read: **A Job with Logs**

Ron has a job. His job is at a big mill. On his job, he has to toss logs on a big, tin box. With an ax and a rig, Ron can do a lot with logs.

Ron is at the bog with his ax and his rig. Big logs are in the bog. Moss is on the logs. Will the logs rot? No, the logs on top will not rot. With his rig, Ron will toss the logs in the box. If the logs do not go, Ron will hit the logs with his ax.

A log jam is at the dam! Can Ron fix it? Ron can do it. That man is fit to do this job. With his ax, Ron hit the logs. He did fix the log jam at the dam.

Ron did fill the big, tin box with logs. Ron did fix the log jam at the dam. The boss nods to him, and he nods to his boss. Will Ron quit this job? No, Ron can do a lot with logs on his job. His job at the big mill is not bad.

At six, Ron and a pal sit at the inn. His pal is Pat. Ron has a bag. He has ham and figs in this bag. His pal, Pat, has yams. Ron will give Pat ham and figs, and Pat will give him yams. A dog is with the pals at the inn. They give the dog a yam. The dog will give Ron and Pat a yip and a kiss.

The pals sit and gab.

Write:

CHAPTER 8:
Words with the ŭ Sound

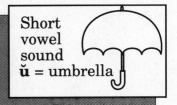

Short vowel sound ŭ = umbrella

SOUNDS

Read: bu   cu   du   fu   gu   hu   ju   lu   mu

       nu   pu   ru   su   tu   vu   yu   zu

Write:

Listen and write:

SOUNDS AND WORDS

Sight Words

Read:

b	bu	bud	but	buff	bug	buzz	bun	bus
c	cu	cub	cud	cuff	cup	cuss	cut	
d	du	dub	dud	dug	dull			
f	fu	fun	fuss	fuzz				
g	gu	gull	gum	gun	Gus	gut		
h	hu	hub	huff	hug	hull	hum	hut	
j	ju	Judd	jug	jut				
l	lu	lug	lull					
m	mu	mud	muff	mug	mull	mum	muss	mutt
n	nu	null	nun	nut				
p	pu	pub	puff	pug	pun	pup	pus	putt
r	ru	rub	ruff	rug	run	Russ	rut	
s	su	sub	sum	sun	sup			
t	tu	tub	tug	tux				
v	vu							
y	yu	yum						
z	zu							
	u	up	us					

come

full

pull, put

some, son

> **Son** sounds like **sun**. **Some** sounds like **sum**.

of

95

WORDS

Read
and
write:

bug {
_____
_____
_____

bus {
_____
_____
_____

cuff {
_____
_____
_____

cut {
_____
_____
_____

cup {
_____
_____
_____

dull {
_____
_____
_____

fun {
_____
_____
_____

gum {
_____
_____
_____

gut {
_____
_____
_____

hug {
_____
_____
_____

jug {
_____
_____
_____

lug {
_____
_____
_____

mud {
_____
_____
_____

nut {
_____
_____
_____

puff {
_____
_____
_____

rub {
_____
_____
_____

rug {
_____
_____
_____

run {
_____
_____
_____

sum {
_____
_____
_____

sun {
_____
_____
_____

tub {
_____
_____
_____

tug {
_____
_____
_____

us {
_____
_____
_____

up {
_____
_____
_____

Listen
and
write:

1. {
_____
_____
_____

7. {
_____
_____
_____

2. {
_____
_____
_____

8. {
_____
_____
_____

3. {
_____
_____
_____

9. {
_____
_____
_____

4. {
_____
_____
_____

10. {
_____
_____
_____

5. {
_____
_____
_____

11. {
_____
_____
_____

6. {
_____
_____
_____

12. {
_____
_____
_____

READ, CIRCLE, WRITE

Read:	Circle the correct picture:	Write:

1. bus mud

2. pup mutt

3. fun run

4. bug rug

5. rub cuff

6. cut nut

7. bun cup

8. lug jug

SENTENCES: STATEMENTS

Read: Write:

1. The bus is in the mud.

2. That pup is a mutt.

3. It is fun to run with him.

4. A bug is in this rug.

5. Rub the mud off the cuff.

6. Russ can cut the nut.

7. He can dip that bun in his cup.

8. Bud and I can lug the jug.

9. The gull sat on the hut.

10. The sun is hot!

11. We had subs and buns.

12. Put the sum on the tag.

Listen and write:

1.

2.

3.

4.

5.

6.

Read: Write:

1. His son is Judd.

2. Rub the fuzz off the rug.

3. Sit up in the tub.

4. They had some gum.

5. You can tug the cub off the log.

6. The bus has a lot of gas.

7. Pull cups off the top of it.

8. She will run to the bus.

9. Some kids come to the hut.

10. Vans run on and off to mills.

11. That cut is full of pus!

12. The tug will pull the sub.

Listen and write:

1.

2.

3.

4.

5.

6.

7.

SENTENCES: QUESTIONS

These questions use the words **did, will, is, can, have, has, are, am,** and **do.**

Read: Write:

1. Did Russ cut the bun?

2. Will Judd hug the cub?

3. Is the pup a mutt?

4. Can Bud lug the jug?

5. Do his sons have dull jobs?

6. Has she put a full cup on it?

7. Have Judd and Russ quit?

8. Are we in a rut?

9. Did it huff and puff?

10. Will you give us some gum?

11. Is Russ in his tux?

12. Can this bus fit in that hut?

Listen and write:

1.

2.

3.

4.

5.

6.

Read: Write:

1. Do the bug and the ant buzz?

2. Has he quit his job?

3. Am I to pin up the full cuff?

4. Are the nuts in a mug?

5. Did the kid hug his mutt?

6. Will the pup run to the cab?

7. Are you full?

8. Can Judd pass the quiz?

9. Can the tug come and pull a sub?

10. Has the fox dug a pit?

11. Have the cups got a tax?

12. Are they hot in the sun?

Listen and write:

1.

2.

3.

4.

5.

6.

7.

STORY

Read: **The Bus**

Judd has a job. It is on a bus. He is up with the sun. The bus runs on and off to an inn and a mill. The job Judd has is not dull!

Judd ran up the hill to his bus. The run up the hill got Judd to huff and puff. Judd got on the bus and put on his cap. He had to pull up his cuffs. Did Judd gas up the bus? No, the bus had lots of gas.

A big man got on the bus. The man had a bus pass to his job at the mill. The man had his jug and bag with him. The big man put the bag and jug on his lap.

A kid got on the bus. His pals did not come with him. This kid had a lot of gum and got some on the big man. The man got so mad at the kid that he got up and ran off the bus. Judd got mad at the kid, but Judd did not fuss. The kid is not his son.

The man got a cab to go to his job at the mill. The man sat in the cab and put his jug and bag on his lap. With the big man, the cab is full!

The cab cut off the bus. It ran the bus in a rut! The bus sat in the mud. Judd got mad and did fuss!

The man in the cab got a van. The van will pull and tug the bus. With six big pulls, the van did it. The bus can run. Judd is not mad.

Will Judd quit his job on the bus? No, he will not quit.

Write:

BONUS PAGE

Read statements:

1. If the tug can pull the sub, it will not sit in the mud.

2. Kim and Judd can have a bit of the hot bun if Jon can cut it.

Write:

1. {
_____
_____

{
_____
_____

2. {
_____
_____

{
_____
_____

Listen and write:

{
_____
_____

{
_____
_____

Read questions:

1. If the tug can pull the sub, will it sit in the mud?

2. Can Kim and Judd have a bit of the hot bun if Jon can cut it?

Write:

1. {
_____
_____

{
_____
_____

2. {
_____
_____

{
_____
_____

Listen and write:

{
_____
_____

{
_____
_____

CHAPTER 9:
Review of the ă, ĭ, ŏ, and ŭ Sounds

SOUNDS

Read:				Write:			
ă	ĭ	ŏ	ŭ	ă	ĭ	ŏ	ŭ
1. ba	bi	bo	bu				
2. ca	-	co	cu				
3. da	di	do	du				
4. fa	fi	fo	fu				
5. ga	gi	go	gu				
6. ha	hi	ho	hu				
7. ja	ji	jo	ju				
8. -	ki	-	-				
9. la	li	lo	lu				
10. ma	mi	mo	mu				
11. na	ni	no	nu				
12. pa	pi	po	pu				
13. -	qui	-	-				
14. ra	ri	ro	ru				
15. sa	si	so	su				
16. ta	ti	to	tu				

17. va   vi   vo   vu   { _____ { _____ { _____ { _____

18. -   wi   -   -   { _____ { _____ { _____ { _____

19. ya   yi   yo   yu   { _____ { _____ { _____ { _____

20. za   zi   zo   zu   { _____ { _____ { _____ { _____

Listen and write (fixed order):

	ă	ĭ	ŏ	ŭ
1.	{ _____	{ _____	{ _____	{ _____
2.	{ _____	{ _____	{ _____	{ _____
3.	{ _____	{ _____	{ _____	{ _____
4.	{ _____	{ _____	{ _____	{ _____
5.	{ _____	{ _____	{ _____	{ _____
6.	{ _____	{ _____	{ _____	{ _____
7.	{ _____	{ _____	{ _____	{ _____
8.	{ _____	{ _____	{ _____	{ _____
9.	{ _____	{ _____	{ _____	{ _____
10.	{ _____	{ _____	{ _____	{ _____

Listen and write (mixed order):

1.	{ _____	{ _____	{ _____	{ _____
2.	{ _____	{ _____	{ _____	{ _____
3.	{ _____	{ _____	{ _____	{ _____
4.	{ _____	{ _____	{ _____	{ _____

SOUND WORDS

Read: Write:

	ă	ĭ	ŏ	ŭ		ă	ĭ	ŏ	ŭ
1.	bag	bit	Bob	bum					
2.	cat	-	cot	cup					
3.	dam	dip	dog	dug					
4.	fat	fig	fog	fun					
5.	gas	gill	got	gum					
6.	hat	hip	hog	hut					
7.	jam	Jim	job	jug					
8.	-	Kim	-	-					
9.	lap	lit	log	lug					
10.	map	mitt	mob	mud					
11.	nap	nip	not	nut					
12.	pal	pin	pot	pup					
13.	-	quit	-	-					
14.	ran	rip	rot	run					
15.	sad	sip	sop	sun					
16.	tan	tip	top	tub					
17.	van	Vin	Von	-					
18.	-	wig	-	-					

19. yam   yip   yon   yum

20. zap   zip   -   -

Listen and write (fixed order):

ă	ĭ	ŏ	ŭ
1.			
2.			
3.			
4.			
5.			
6.			
7.			
8.			
9.			
10.			

Listen and write (mixed order):

1.			
2.			
3.			
4.			
5.			

SIGHT WORDS

Read: Write:

1. give   Give

2. live   Live

3. have   Have

4. the   The

5. a   A

6. I   I

7. you   You

8. they   They

9. are   Are

10. no   No

11. go   Go

12. so   So

Read: **Write:**

13. to   To

14. do   Do

15. full   Full

16. pull   Pull

17. put   Put

18. son   Son

19. some   Some

20. come   Come

21. of   Of

22. he   He

23. she   She

24. we   We

25. be   Be

Listen and write (sight words):

1.
2.
3.
4.
5.
6.
7.
8.
9.
10.

Listen and write (sound words and sight words):

1.
2.
3.
4.
5.
6.
7.
8.

SENTENCES: STATEMENTS

Read and write:

1. Bob and I put a bit of gum in his bag.

   ----

2. If the pup has a nap, it will not nip.

   ----

3. They can put the log on top so it will not rot.

   ----

4. You can fill the tub up to the top and sit in it.

   ----

5. The cubs can run with us on top of that hill.

   ----

6. Vin has a van, but Von has a bus.

   ----

7. The kids run on and off this tug.

   ----

8. At his job, Russ has to put pins in the cuffs.

   ----

9. She will pull the mutt off the big, tan mat.

   ----

10. We got some mud on the big van, and the man is in a huff.

    ----

11. The hat is tan, but the tux is not.

    ----

12. He will sip the fizz off the top of the mug.

SENTENCES: QUESTIONS

Read and write:

1. Will they quit the bad job in a huff?

2. Can we fit the big tub in the van?

3. Did the man and his son have a tan cab?

4. On the hill, do we have six cats and some dogs?

5. If he has a map, can he run to the mill?

6. Will you mix some nuts in a can for us?

7. Did Dad have you fill the cups up to the rims?

8. Are you as full as I am?

9. This cap is big, but is that cap as big as this?

10. Did the tot give the dolls a hug and a kiss?

11. Can Max, Roz, and I come up that hill in a van?

12. Will she add the tax on this bill?

Listen and write:

1. {
_____
_____

2. {
_____
_____

3. {
_____
_____

4. {
_____
_____

5. {
_____
_____

6. {
_____
_____

7. {
_____
_____

8. {
_____
_____

9. {
_____
_____

10. {
_____
_____

11. {
_____
_____

12. {
_____
_____

13. {
_____
_____

14. {
_____
_____

15. {
_____
_____

16. {
_____
_____

17. {
_____
_____

18. {
_____
_____

STORY

Read: **The Job at the Gull Inn**

    Kim has a job. It is not a bad job. It is at the Gull Inn. He can live at the inn. On the job, Kim can have a lot of tips. He puts on a tux with a tan mum in it.

    But Kim has a lot to do on the job. He has to mop. He has to buff the dull pots with a rag. To buff, he has to dip his rag in a hot pot. He has to lug big jugs and a big box. Kim has to put the tops on the pans and the lids on the pots. He has to fill the cups with nuts.

    A man and six kids sat in the inn. Kim had to give them big subs, lots of ribs, buns with jam, and mugs of pop. He had to add up the bill, add on the tax, and put the sum on his pad. He got a big tip.

    Kim has a bad boss. The boss nags him a lot. Will Kim quit? No, he will not quit. He has lots of tips, and he has fun on the job.

Write:

CHAPTER 10:
Words with the ĕ Sound

Short
vowel
sound
ĕ = egg

SOUNDS

Read: be   de   fe   ge   he   je   ke   le   me   ne

pe   que   re   se   te   ve   we   ye   ze

Write: {

Listen
and {
write:

{

SOUNDS AND WORDS

Read:

b	be	bed	beg	bell	Ben	Bess	bet	
d	de	dell	den					
f	fe	fed	fell	fen				
g	ge	get						
h	he	hem	hen	hex				
j	je	Jeb	Jed	Jeff	jell	Jen	Jess	jet
k	ke	keg	Ken	Kev				
l	le	led	leg	Len	Les	less	let	
m	me	Meg	Mel	men	mess	met		
n	ne	Ned	Nell	net				
p	pe	peg	Peg	pen	pep	pet		
qu	que	quell						
r	re	red	Rex					
s	se	sell	set	sex				
t	te	Ted	tell	ten				
v	ve	vex						
w	we	web	wed	well	Wes	wet		
y	ye	yell	yen	yes	yet			
z	ze	Zen						

Sight Words

be

he, her

me

she, said

we

WORDS

Read
and
write: bed {

den {

fell {

hen {

jet {

leg {

mess {

pen {

red {

ten {

web {

yet {

beg {

fed {

get {

Jeff {

Ken {

men {

net {

quell {

sell {

vex {

wed {

Zen {

Listen
and
write: 1. {

2. {

3. {

4. {

5. {

6. {

7. {

8. {

9. {

10. {

11. {

12. {

READ, CIRCLE, WRITE

Read:	Circle the correct picture:	Write:

1. ten men

2. bell well

3. hen egg

4. wet net

5. bed mess

6. pet beg

7. fell leg

8. sell jet

SIGHT WORDS: He/he, She/she, Me/me, We/we, Be/be

Read: He   he   She   she   Me   me   We   we   Be   be   Me   We

he   she   me   we   be   He   She   Me   We   Be   she   he

Write: {

Read sentences: Write:

1. **Dan** runs.

2. **He** runs.

3. **Nan** sits.

4. **She** sits.

5. **Peg and I** met.

6. **We** met.

7. **I** fed it.

8. Give it to **me.**

9. Did he fix the bus?

10. Can she run to the top?

11. Will we be at the inn?

12. Will Meg give me a map?

Listen and write:

1. {   3. {

2. {   4. {

SIGHT WORD: her, Her

Compare **his** and **her.**

Read: her   Her   her   Her   her   Her   her   Her   her   Her   her   Her
          her   his   Her   His   her   his   Her   His   her   his   Her   His

Write:

Read sentences: Write:

  1. This is Nan.

  2. This is her dog.

  3. This is Tim.

  4. This is his dog.

  5. She ran to her mom.

  6. She ran to her dad.

  7. He ran to his mom.

  8. He ran to his dad.

  9. Jill has her cap.

 10. Don has his hat.

 11. Meg ran to her bus.

 12. Russ sat in his van.

Listen and write:

1.   3.

2.   4.

SENTENCES: STATEMENTS

Read: Write:

1. Ten men met Ben and Meg.

2. The bell fell in the well.

3. That red hen has eggs.

4. Jed has no pep and is in bed.

5. Jeff bet Len the red pen.

6. I said, "Get less gas."

7. This pen set is not red.

8. Nell said, "Sell the jet."

9. Let Wes sell the ten pets.

10. He is not ill. He is well.

11. Yes, she did yell at me.

12. They met them at the inn.

Listen and write:

1.

2.

3.

4.

5.

6.

Read: Write:

1. Jed wed Jen in the dell.

2. Ted put his pet in the den.

3. Bess met Rex at the well.

4. You have a pet hen.

5. We had the vet set the leg.

6. The jam will jell then.

7. The hen led me to the mess.

8. She will sell me her net.

9. Tell Ken to let me hem it.

10. The wet bug is in the web.

11. He will be at the jet.

12. Wes has a bed in his den.

Listen and write:

1.

2.

3.

4.

5.

6.

7.

SENTENCES: QUESTIONS AND ANSWERS

These questions use the words **did, will, is, can, have, has, are, am,** and **do.**
Compare the **yes** and **no** answers.

Read: Write:

1. Did he get that red hen yet?

2. Yes, he did. He got that hen.

3. Will Jen sell this jet?

4. No, she will not.

5. Is her bed a mess?

6. Yes, her bed is a mess.

7. Can Rex hem his net at ten?

8. No, he cannot do it then.

9. "Meg, do you sell bells?"

10. "Yes, I do sell them."

11. Has the vet fed her pets?

12. No, she has not fed them.

Listen and write:

1.

2.

3.

4.

5.

6.

Read: Write:

1. Have Wen and Meg met yet?

2. Yes, they have.

3. Are we at the red mill?

4. No, we are at the well.

5. Did you and Wes tell Ben?

6. Yes, we did tell him.

7. Will they yell at you?

8. No, they will not yell at me.

9. Len said, "Mom, is it ten yet?"

10. Mom said, "Yes, son, it is."

11. Can Peg get less gas?

12. No, she cannot.

Listen and write:

1.

2.

3.

4.

5.

6.

STORY

Read: **Beth and Her Red Hen**

Beth has ten hens. They are not pets. She has the hens to get eggs. She will sell the eggs to inns.

Her red hen is a bad hen. It did not give her eggs. This hen did vex her! She is fed up with it. Beth said, "I will get rid of it. I will sell it! I will not put it off. I will not miss that bad hen."

Will she sell the hen to an inn? Yes, she will. At the inn, the men will kill the hen. They will cut it up, put it in a hot pot, and mix it with some dill.

Beth did not sell the red hen yet. She will go to the inn to sell the hen. Beth will have her pet dog, Rex, with her. She put the hen in a net bag. "Let us go, Rex," Beth said, "but do not mess with this bag. I will get mad and yell at you if you do!"

At the inn, Rex is bad. He got the bag with the hen in it and ran. The bag fell in a big well with a bell on top of it. The red hen got wet. It got up and ran. Beth and her pet, Rex, ran to get the hen, but the hen ran and hid. "A hex on you!" said Beth. To get the red hen to come to her, Beth fed it a cob. With the cob, she got the hen.

Beth put the red hen in a pen at the inn. The men, Jeff and Ted, met her and said, "That hen is full of pep. It did well. We bet it will be a fun pet. Sell us the red hen as a pet, and we will give you ten big bills."

Beth sat. She had had it! She had her pet dog, Rex, and ten big bills. Jeff and Ted had a pet, the red hen.

Write:

BONUS PAGE

Read statements:

1. If she cannot get gas, she will sell the jet.

2. You will not get eggs if you have that red hen.

Write:

1. {
_____

2. {
_____

Listen and write:

{
_____

{
_____

Read questions:

1. If she cannot get gas, will she sell the jet?

2. Will you get eggs if you have that red hen?

Write:

1. {
_____

2. {
_____

Listen and write:

{
_____

{
_____

CHAPTER 11:
Review of the ă, ĕ, ĭ, ŏ, and ŭ Sounds

SOUNDS

Read:

	ă	ĕ	ĭ	ŏ	ŭ
1.	ba	be	bi	bo	bu
2.	ca	-	-	co	cu
3.	da	de	di	do	du
4.	fa	fe	fi	fo	fu
5.	ga	ge	gi	go	gu
6.	ha	he	hi	ho	hu
7.	ja	je	ji	jo	ju
8.	-	ke	ki	-	-
9.	la	le	li	lo	lu
10.	ma	me	mi	mo	mu
11.	na	ne	ni	no	nu
12.	pa	pe	pi	po	pu
13.	-	que	qui	-	-
14.	ra	re	ri	ro	ru
15.	sa	se	si	so	su
16.	ta	te	ti	to	tu

Write:

ă   ĕ   ĭ   ŏ   ŭ

17. va   ve   vi   vo   vu

18. -   we   wi   -   -

19. ya   ye   yi   yo   yu

20. za   ze   zi   zo   zu

Listen and write (fixed order):

ă   ĕ   ĭ   ŏ   ŭ

1.

2.

3.

4.

5.

6.

7.

8.

9.

10.

Listen and write (mixed order):

1.

2.

3.

SOUND WORDS

Read: Write:

	ă	ĕ	ĭ	ŏ	ŭ	ă	ĕ	ĭ	ŏ	ŭ
1.	bag	beg	big	bog	bug					
2.	cat	-	-	cot	cut					
3.	dad	den	did	Don	dug					
4.	fat	fed	fig	fog	fun					
5.	gas	get	gill	got	gun					
6.	hat	hen	hill	hot	hut					
7.	jam	jet	jib	jog	jug					
8.	-	keg	kit	-	-					
9.	lap	leg	lip	log	lug					
10.	map	men	miss	mop	mud					
11.	nap	net	nip	nod	nut					
12.	pal	peg	pin	pot	pup					
13.	-	quell	quit	-	-					
14.	ran	red	rip	rot	run					
15.	sad	set	sip	sop	sun					
16.	tan	ten	tip	top	tub					
17.	van	vet	Vin	Von	-					
18.	-	wet	wig	-	-					

19. yam   yet   yip   yon   yum   {_____ {_____ {_____ {_____ {_____

20. zap   Zen   zip   -   -   {_____ {_____ {_____ {_____ {_____

Listen and write (fixed order):

	ă	ĕ	ĭ	ŏ	ŭ
1.	{_____	{_____	{_____	{_____	{_____
2.	{_____	{_____	{_____	{_____	{_____
3.	{_____	{_____	{_____	{_____	{_____
4.	{_____	{_____	{_____	{_____	{_____
5.	{_____	{_____	{_____	{_____	{_____
6.	{_____	{_____	{_____	{_____	{_____
7.	{_____	{_____	{_____	{_____	{_____
8.	{_____	{_____	{_____	{_____	{_____
9.	{_____	{_____	{_____	{_____	{_____
10.	{_____	{_____	{_____	{_____	{_____

Listen and write (mixed order):

1.	{_____	{_____	{_____	{_____	{_____
2.	{_____	{_____	{_____	{_____	{_____
3.	{_____	{_____	{_____	{_____	{_____
4.	{_____	{_____	{_____	{_____	{_____
5.	{_____	{_____	{_____	{_____	{_____

SIGHT WORDS

Read: Write:

1. give   Give

2. live   Live

3. have   Have

4. the   The

5. a   A

6. I   I

7. you   You

8. they   They

9. are   Are

10. no   No

11. go   Go

12. so   So

13. to   To

14. do   Do

Read: Write:

15. full   Full

16. pull   Pull

17. put   Put

18. son   Son

19. some   Some

20. come   Come

21. of   Of

22. me   Me

23. he   He

24. she   She

25. we   We

26. be   Be

27. her   Her

28. said   Said

Listen and write (sight words):

1.

2.

3.

4.

5.

6.

7.

8.

9.

10.

Listen and write (sound words and sight words):

1.

2.

3.

4.

5.

6.

7.

8.

SENTENCES: STATEMENTS

Read and write:

1. The ax is dull, so it will not cut well.

   ----

2. He said, "I am the boss at a big mill."

   ----

3. She put a full mug and some cut buns on her mat.

   ----

4. No, Bud will not come and live with Ken and me.

   ----

5. We fell in the well and got wet, but we are not mad.

   ----

6. You are the man to do the job in this lab!

   ----

7. They did tell us a fib, but they are not bad kids.

   ----

8. I met Judd on the bus, and then I met his son.

   ----

9. Six bugs are in that web.

   ----

10. Some of us will pull the logs up the hill with them.

    ----

11. Yes, she has a map and will go to the inn at ten.

    ----

12. At the vet, the mutt will sit up and beg.

SENTENCES: QUESTIONS

Read and write:

1. Will Dad have me fill his cup to the rim?

2. Can Miss Lin and Kim wed at the Red Inn?

3. Are the cuffs on the tux yet?

4. Has the dog dug a pit in the hill? Was it a bad mess?

5. If her tan mugs have a tax, then will her red cups have a tax?

6. "Will the sad tot fuss in the tub?" she said to Miss Yap.

7. Are ten gulls on the hut with him? Is he in a jam?

8. Can Russ, Pat, and he mix up the nuts in this pot?

9. Is the big boss in the lab at the mill with them?

10. He said to his pal, "Will the kids give us some gum?"

11. If you and I run up to the top of that hill, will we huff and puff?

12. Will they cut the ten hot buns if we fill the six tan mugs?

Listen and write:

1. {

2. {

3. {

4. {

5. {

6. {

7. {

8. {

9. {

10. {

11. {

12. {

13. {

14. {

15. {

16. {

17. {

18. {

STORY

Read: **Did Mom, Dad, and the Kids Have Fun?**

<u>The Big Ad</u>

The Jet Set ran a big ad. The ad said, "Lots to sell! Come and get it!"

Mom said to Dad, "It is not a bad ad." They will go to the Jet Set.

Dad said, "The kids can come with us. We will have fun at the Jet Set. Then we will go to the Gull Inn."

Mom and Dad said to the kids, "Will you go with us to the Jet Set and the Gull Inn?"

"Yes!" the kids said. "Can we go on the bus? Can we go in a cab?"

Dad said, "No, we will go in the van. We have a map to the Jet Set. So let us get in the van and go."

<u>At the Jet Set</u>

At the Jet Set, Mom, Dad, and the kids got a lot. They got a big bed with a pad, a cot that was not big, a red rug, and a tan mat to go in the tub. They got some pots and pans with lids, some cups, and a set of ten mugs.

Mom and the kids got a mop, some pins to put up hems, a bell that can buzz, and a lot of rags to wax the van and buff the pots. Dad and the kids got an ax to cut logs. This ax is not dull!

Ben put on a tan cap, and it fit him. He got it. Ann put on a red hat, but it did not fit her. She did not get it. The red hat is less than the tan cap, so Ann got mad. Dad put on a tux, but the cuff had a bad rip. Will Mom fix it? No, she will not. Can Dad fix it? No, so Dad will not get the tux. But Jill got six red pens.

The big ad did not tell a fib. At the Jet Set, they did have lots to sell. And they got a lot! A man put some of it in a big box and some of it in bags. That is his job at the Jet Set.

"Give me the big box," said Dad, "but give the kids the bags. We will put them in the van."

Mom said, "The van will be so full!"

The man at the Jet Set had the bill. He did add the tax. The tag on the red

rug did not have a tax. With the tax, it is a big sum. But Mom and Dad had the

sum. Dad had his pen, and Mom had the bill.

Is it dull at the Jet Set? No, it is fun at the Jet Set!

At the Gull Inn

"Can we fit in the van with this big box and the bags? Can we go to the Gull

Inn?" Dad said.

"Yes, we can do it," Mom said. "We are not that fat."

So the kids, Dad, and Mom got in the full van. They had a map and got to

the Gull Inn. At the Gull Inn, Mom had cod on a bun. Dad had ham with some yams.

Jill had ten ribs.

Ben said to Jill, "Will you cut some ribs and give them to me?"

"Yes, Ben," Jill said, "I will cut the ribs and give some to you."

The kids had subs and six cans of pop. The pop had a lot of fizz. They had

lots of jam on buns. Then the kids had some gum, and Mom and Dad had nuts and

figs. They had lots and lots. Are they fat? Not yet! They are thin, but they are full.

Can Mom, Dad, and the kids fit in the van with the big box and the bags?

Yes, they can. Did they have fun at the Gull Inn? Yes, they did. They had a lot of

fun at the Gull Inn!

Write:

_____
_____

_____
_____

_____
_____

_____
_____

UNIT THREE:
Life Skills

In Chapters 12, 13, and 14, you will read and write

▶ numbers

▶ colors

▶ personal identification

CHAPTER 12:
Numbers

COUNTING SUMMARY CHART: 0–100

Read:

0	10	20	30	40	50	60	70	80	90	100
1	11	21	31	41	51	61	71	81	91	
2	12	22	32	42	52	62	72	82	92	
3	13	23	33	43	53	63	73	83	93	
4	14	24	34	44	54	64	74	84	94	
5	15	25	35	45	55	65	75	85	95	
6	16	26	36	46	56	66	76	86	96	
7	17	27	37	47	57	67	77	87	97	
8	18	28	38	48	58	68	78	88	98	
9	19	29	39	49	59	69	79	89	99	

DIGITS: 0–9

Read and write:

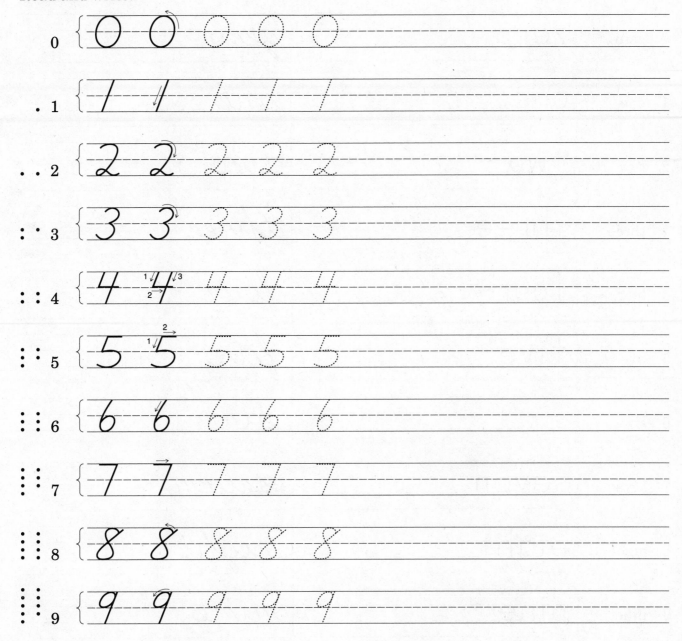

NUMBER NAMES: 0–9

Read:	Print:	Write:
0 zero	zero	zero
1 one	one	one
2 two	two	two
3 three	three	three
4 four	four	four
5 five	five	five
6 six	six	six
7 seven	seven	seven
8 eight	eight	eight
9 nine	nine	nine

NUMBER NAMES: 10–19

Read:	Print:	Write:
10 ten	ten	ten
11 eleven	eleven	eleven
12 twelve	twelve	twelve
13 thirteen	thirteen	thirteen
14 fourteen	fourteen	fourteen
15 fifteen	fifteen	fifteen
16 sixteen	sixteen	sixteen
17 seventeen	seventeen	seventeen
18 eighteen	eighteen	eighteen
19 nineteen	nineteen	nineteen

NUMBER NAMES: 20–29

Read: | Print: | Write:

	Read:	Print:	Write:
20	twenty	twenty	twenty
21	twenty-one	twenty-one	twenty-one
22	twenty-two	twenty-two	twenty-two
23	twenty-three	twenty-three	twenty-three
24	twenty-four	twenty-four	twenty-four
25	twenty-five	twenty-five	twenty-five
26	twenty-six	twenty-six	twenty-six
27	twenty-seven	twenty-seven	twenty-seven
28	twenty-eight	twenty-eight	twenty-eight
29	twenty-nine	twenty-nine	twenty-nine

NUMBER NAMES: 30–90

Read: Print:

30 thirty   { thirty

40 forty   { forty

50 fifty   { fifty

60 sixty   { sixty

70 seventy { seventy

80 eighty   { eighty

90 ninety   { ninety

Write:

{ thirty

{ forty

{ fifty

{ sixty

{ seventy

{ eighty

{ ninety

NUMBER NAMES: SELECTED (100–1,000,000,000)

Read: Print:

100
one hundred   one hundred

1,000
one thousand   one thousand

10,000
ten thousand   ten thousand

100,000
one hundred thousand   one hundred thousand

1,000,000
one million   one million

1,000,000,000
one billion   one billion

Write:

one hundred

one thousand

ten thousand

one hundred thousand

one million

one billion

THE CALENDAR

December, 19____						
Sunday	Monday	Tuesday	Wednesday	Thursday	Friday	Saturday
1	2	3	4	5	6	7
8	9	10	11	12	13	14
15	16	17	18	19	20	21
22	23	24	25	26	27	28
29	30	31				

The Days of the Week

Read: Write:

Sunday

Monday

Tuesday

Wednesday

Thursday

Friday

Saturday

Abbreviations

Read: Write:

Sun.

Mon.

Tues.

Wed.

Thurs.

Fri.

Sat.

The Months of the Year

Read: Write:

January   {_____
             _____

February   {_____
             _____

March   {_____
             _____

April   {_____
             _____

May   {_____
             _____

June   {_____
             _____

July   {_____
             _____

August   {_____
             _____

September   {_____
             _____

October   {_____
             _____

November   {_____
             _____

December   {_____
             _____

Abbreviations

Read: Write:

Jan.   {_____
         _____

Feb.   {_____
         _____

Mar.   {_____
         _____

Apr.   {_____
         _____

May   {_____
         _____

June   {_____
         _____

July   {_____
         _____

Aug.   {_____
         _____

Sept.   {_____
         _____

Oct.   {_____
         _____

Nov.   {_____
         _____

Dec.   {_____
         _____

THE CLOCK: TELLING TIME

What time is it?

> A.M. is used with times in the morning (from midnight to noon).

Read: Write:

It's 1:00 A.M.

It's one A.M.

It's one o'clock in the morning.

It's 2:15 A.M.

It's two fifteen A.M.*

It's two fifteen in the morning.*

It's a quarter past two in the morning.

It's a quarter after two in the morning.

It's 3:30 A.M.

It's three thirty A.M.*

It's three thirty in the morning.*

It's half past** three in the morning.

---

*In these sentences, the times have been written out in words to indicate how they should be pronounced. Normally, time is written in numerals, as shown in the first example for each time.

Note that *after* can be used in place of *past* in all cases **except *half past*.

What time is it?

Read: Write:

It's 4:45 A.M.

It's four forty-five A.M.*

It's four forty-five in the morning.*

It's a quarter to** five in the morning.

It's 5:05 A.M.

It's five-o-five A.M.*

It's five-o-five in the morning.*

It's five minutes past five in the morning.

It's 6:40 A.M.

It's six forty A.M.*

It's six forty in the morning.*

It's twenty minutes to seven in the morning.

---

*In these sentences, the times have been written out in words to indicate how they
  should be pronounced. Normally, time is written in numerals, as shown in the first
  example for each time.

**Note that *of* can be used in place of *to*. For example: It's twenty minutes of seven
  in the morning.

What time is it?

Read: Write:

It's 7:23 A.M.

It's seven twenty-three A.M.*

It's seven twenty-three in the morning.*

It's twenty-three minutes past seven in the morning.

It's 8:54 A.M.

It's eight fifty-four A.M.*

It's eight fifty-four in the morning.*

It's six minutes to nine in the morning.

It's noon.

It's 12:00 noon.**

It's noontime.

It's twelve noon.

It's midday.

---

*In these sentences, the times have been written out in words to indicate how they should be pronounced. Normally, time is written in numerals, as shown in the first example for each time.

**12:00 noon is neither A.M. nor P.M. It is 12:00 M. Compare 11:59 A.M., 12:00 M., and 12:01 P.M. 12:00 midnight is 12:00 P.M.

What time is it?

> P.M. is used with times in the afternoon, in the evening, and at night (from noon to midnight).

Read: Write:

It's 5:45 P.M.

It's five forty-five P.M.*

It's five forty-five in the afternoon.*

It's a quarter to six in the afternoon.

It's a quarter to six in the evening.

It's 6:09 P.M.

It's six-o-nine P.M.*

It's six-o-nine in the evening.*

It's nine minutes past six in the evening.

It's 9:17 P.M.

It's nine seventeen P.M.*

It's nine seventeen in the evening.*

It's seventeen minutes past nine at night.**

---

*In these sentences, the times have been written out in words to indicate how they should be pronounced. Normally, time is written in numerals, as shown in the first example for each time.

**Note that *in the evening* can be used in place of *at night*.

What time is it?

Read: Write:

It's 10:38 P.M.

It's ten thirty-eight P.M.*

It's ten thirty-eight at night.*

It's twenty-two minutes to eleven at night.

It's 11:46 P.M.

It's eleven forty-six P.M.*

It's eleven forty-six at night.*

It's fourteen minutes to twelve at night.

It's midnight.

It's 12:00 midnight.

It's twelve midnight.

It's twelve o'clock at night.

*In these sentences, the times have been written out in words to indicate how they
 should be pronounced. Normally, time is written in numerals, as shown in the first
 example for each time.

TIME EXERCISES

Write the numbers and the words you would say:

1. I wake up at { *seven o'clock in the morning.*
   7:00 A.M.

2. I have breakfast at {

3. I leave my house at {

4. I catch the bus at {

5. I start working at {

6. I have lunch at {

7. I leave work at {

8. I have dinner at {

9. I go to sleep at {

Read: **Write what you would say:**

1:00 A.M.   { *one o'clock in the morning*

3:30 P.M.   {

6:15 P.M.   {

7:45 P.M.   {

12 noon   {

12 midnight   {

5:17 A.M.   {

8:29 P.M.   {

4:51 A.M.   {

2:04 P.M.   {

9:35 A.M.   {

Read: **Write the time in numbers:**

It's three o'clock in the morning.   { *It's 3:00 A.M.*

It's four-thirty in the afternoon.   {

It's a quarter after five in the morning.   {

It's a quarter to nine at night.   {

It's ten after seven in the morning.   {

It's twenty minutes to eight in the evening.   {

It's midnight.   {

CHAPTER 13:
Colors

Read: **Print:**

○ red { red

○ yellow { yellow

○ blue { blue

○ orange { orange

○ green { green

○ purple { purple

Write:

{ red

{ yellow

{ blue

{ orange

{ green

{ purple

Read: Print:

◯ black   { black

◯ white   { white

◯ brown   { brown

◯ tan   { tan

◯ gray   { gray

◯ pink   { pink

Write:

{ black

{ white

{ brown

{ tan

{ gray

{ pink

CHAPTER 14:
Personal Identification

ABBREVIATIONS

Titles

Read:	(Full Spelling)	Write:	Example:
1. Mr.	(Mister)		Mr. Jones
2. Mrs.			Mrs. Smith
3. Ms.			Ms. Ross
4. Miss			Miss Lee
5. Dr.	(Doctor)		Dr. John Kim
6. Ph.D.	(Doctor of Philosophy)		John Kim, Ph.D. (Dr. John Kim)
7. M.D.	(Medical Doctor)		John Kim, M.D. (Dr. John Kim)
8. D.D.S.	(Doctor of Dental Surgery)		John Kim, D.D.S. (Dr. John Kim)
9. D.M.D.	(Doctor of Dental Medicine)		John Kim, D.M.D. (Dr. John Kim)
10. Prof.	(Professor)		Prof. Tong
11. Jr.	(Junior)		David Ford, Jr.

Places

Read:	(Full Spelling)	Write:	Example:
1. St.	(Street)		12 Main St.
2. Ave.	(Avenue)		5 Elm Ave.
3. Rd.	(Road)		4 Haven Rd.
4. U.S.A.	(United States of America)		
5. P.O. Box	(Post Office Box)		P.O. Box 76

Other

Read: (Full Spelling)   Write:

1. S.S.#   (Social Security Number)

2. Phone No.   (Telephone Number)

3. M/F   (Male or Female)

4. Co.   (Company)

5. Inc.   (Incorporated)

6. C.O.D.   (Cash on Delivery)

7. UPS   (United Parcel Service)

8. Acct. #   (Account Number)

9. lb.   (pound)

10. wt.   (weight)

11. ht.   (height)

12. GI   (Government Issue—member of U.S. Armed Forces)

13. NASA   (National Aeronautics and Space Administration)

Write:

1.

2.

3.

4.

ANSWERING QUESTIONS

What is your name?

My name is

Print (using upper-case and lower-case letters):

Example: { Karen   Ellen   Smith
           First Name   Middle Name   Last Name

1. {
   First Name   Middle Name   Last Name

2. {
   First Name   Middle Name   Last Name

Print (using all capitals):

Example: { SMITH   KAREN   E.
           Last Name   First Name   Middle Initial

3. {
   Last Name   First Name   Middle Initial

4. {
   Last Name   First Name   Middle Initial

Write:

Example: { Karen   Ellen   Smith
           First Name   Middle Name   Last Name

5. {
   First Name   Middle Name   Last Name

6. {
   First Name   Middle Name   Last Name

What country do you come from?

Where are you from?

I come from

What nationality are you?

What are you?

I am

Print (using upper-case and lower-case letters):

Example:

{ Mexico

{ Mexican

1. {

2. {

Print (using all capitals):

Example:

{ MEXICO

{ MEXICAN

3. {

4. {

Write:

Example:

{ Mexico

{ Mexican

5. {

6. {

What is your address?

My address is

Print (using upper-case and lower-case letters):

Example: { *12 Main St.*
Street

{ *Topeka,*   *KS*   *66600*
City   State   Zip Code

1. {

{

2. {

{

Print (using all capitals):

Example: { *12 MAIN ST.*
Street

{ *TOPEKA,*   *KS*   *66600*
City   State   Zip Code

3. {

{

Write:

Example: { *12 Main St.*
Street

{ *Topeka,*   *KS*   *66600*
City   State   Zip Code

4. {

{

What is your telephone number?

What is your social security number?

My telephone number is

My social security number is

Example: My telephone number is { (*198*) *555-2637* .

My social security number is { *123-45-6789* .

1. My telephone number is { ( ) .

My social security number is { .

2. My telephone number is { ( ) .

My social security number is { .

3. My telephone number is { ( ) .

My social security number is { .

4. My telephone number is { ( ) .

My social security number is { .

5. My telephone number is { ( ) .

My social security number is { .

What is your job (occupation)?

What do you do?

I am a/an

Print (using lower-case letters):

Example: carpenter

1.

2.

3.

Print (using all capitals):

Example: CARPENTER

4.

5.

6.

Write:

Example: carpenter

7.

8.

9.

Appendix A:
Scope and Sequence Charts

▶ Parts of Speech for ĭ Words

▶ Parts of Speech for ă Words

▶ Parts of Speech for ŏ Words

▶ Parts of Speech for ŭ Words

▶ Parts of Speech for ĕ Words

SCOPE AND SEQUENCE CHART: PARTS OF SPEECH FOR ĭ WORDS

Proper Nouns	Verbs	Adjectives	Nouns		Pronouns	Prepositions	Other (type)
Bill	bid	big	bid	nil	him	in	if (conjunction)
Gil	bill	dim	bill	nip	his	till	Miss (title)
Jill	bit	ill	bin	nix	it		till (conjunction)
Jim	did	mid	bit	pig			
Kim	dig	six	dill	pill			*the (article)
Kit	dim	tin	din	pin			
Lil	dip		dip	pip			
Lin	fib		fib	pit			
Sid	fill		fig	quid			
Tim	fit		fill	quill			
Vin	fix		fin	quip			
Viv	fizz		fit	quit			
Will	*give		fix	quiz			
Yim	hid		fizz	rib			
Yin	hit		gig	rig			
Yip	is		gill	rill			
	jig		hill	rim			
	kid		hip	rip			
	kill		hit	sill			
	kiss		inn	sin			
	lit		jib	sip			
	*live		jig	six			
	mill		kid	till			
	miss		kin	tin			
	mix		kiss	tip			
	nip		kit	vim			
	nix		lid	wig			
	pin		lip	will			
	pit		mill	wit			
	quip		mitt	wiz			
	quit		mix	yip			
	quiz		nib	zig			

*This is a sight word.

SCOPE AND SEQUENCE CHART: PARTS OF SPEECH FOR ă WORDS

Proper Nouns	Verbs		Adjectives	Nouns		Pronouns	Prepositions	Other (type)
Ann	add	pass	bad	ad	man		at	*a (article)
Dad	am	pat	fat	ant	map			an (article)
Dan	*are	ram	mad	ax	mass			and (conjunction)
Jan	ax	ran	sad	bag	mat			
Matt	bag	rap	tan	ban	nag			as (conjunction)
Max	ban	rat		bat	nap			
Nan	bat	sag		cab	pad			
Pam	can	sap		cad	pal			
Pat	cap	sass		cam	pan			
Sal	dab	sat		can	pass			
Sam	dam	tab		cap	pat			
Val	fan	tag		cat	rag			
Van	gab	tan		dab	ram			
Yam	gad	tap		dad	rap			
Yan	gag	tax		dam	rat			
Yap	gap	yak		fad	sag			
	gas	yap		fan	sap			
	had	zag		fat	tab			
	has	zap		gag	tag			
	*have			gal	tam			
	jab			gap	tan			
	jam			gas	tax			
	lag			hag	van			
	lap			ham	vat			
	man			hat	yak			
	map			jab	yam			
	mat			jag	yap			
	nab			jam	zag			
	nag			lab				
	nap			lad				
	pad			lap				
	pan			lass				

*This is a sight word.

SCOPE AND SEQUENCE CHART: PARTS OF SPEECH FOR ŏ WORDS

Proper Nouns	Verbs	Adjectives	Pronouns	Nouns		Prepositions	Other (type)
Bob	bob	hot		bog	pox	off	off (adverb, adjective)
Don	bog	mod		bop	rod	on	on (adverb, adjective)
Dot	bop	top		boss	rot	*to	
Jon	boss	yon		box	sob		*no (adverb, adjective)
Lon	box			cob	sod		
Mom	con			cod	sop		non (prefix)
Pop	cop			cog	sot		not (adverb)
Rob	*do			con	top		*so (adverb, conjunction)
Rod	dot			cop	toss		
Ron	fox			cot	tot		yon (adverb, adjective)
Roz	*go			dog			
Todd	got			doll			
Tom	hog			dot			
Von	hop			fog			
	jog			fox			
	jot			gob			
	lob			hog			
	log			hop			
	lop			job			
	mob			jot			
	mop			lob			
	nod			log			
	pop			loss			
	pot			lot			
	rob			mob			
	rot			mom			
	sob			mop			
	sod			moss			
	sop			nod			
	top			pod			
	toss			pop			
				pot			

*This is a sight word.

SCOPE AND SEQUENCE CHART: PARTS OF SPEECH FOR ŭ WORDS

Proper Nouns	Verbs	Adjectives	Nouns	Pronouns	Prepositions	Other (type)
Bud	bud	dull	bud / mug	us	*of	but (conjunction)
Buzz	buff	*full	bug / mum		up	up (adverb)
Judd	bug	fun	bum / mutt			yum (interjection)
Mum	bum	mum	bun / nun			
Russ	bus	null	bus / nut			
	butt	*some	butt / pub			
	buzz		buzz / puff			
	*come		cub / pug			
	cuff		cud / *pull			
	cup		cuff / pun			
	cuss		cup / pup			
	cut		cuss / pus			
	dub		cut / putt			
	dug		dud / rub			
	dull		fun / ruff			
	fuss		fuss / rug			
	gum		fuzz / run			
	gun		gull / rut			
	gut		gum / *son			
	huff		gun / sub			
	hug		gut / sum			
	hull		hub / sun			
	hum		huff / tub			
	jut		hug / tug			
	lug		hull / tux			
	lull		hum			
	mug		hut			
	mull		jug			
	muss		lug			
	puff		lull			
	*pull		mud			
	pun		muff			
	*put					
	putt					
	rub					
	run					
	sum					
	sun					
	sup					
	tug					

*This is a sight word.

SCOPE AND SEQUENCE CHART: PARTS OF SPEECH FOR ĕ WORDS

Proper Nouns	Verbs	Adjectives	Nouns	Pronouns	Prepositions	Other (type)
Ben	*be	less	bed	*he		less (adverb)
Bess	bed	red	bell	*her		well (adverb, interjection)
Jeb	beg	ten	bet	*me		
Jed	bet	wet	dell	*we		yes (adverb)
Jeff	fed	well	den	*she		yet (adverb, conjunction)
Jen	fell		fen			
Jess	get		hem			
Ken	hem		hen			
Kev	hex		hex			
Len	jell		jell			
Les	jet		jet			
Meg	led		keg			
Mel	let		leg			
Ned	mess		men			
Nell	met		mess			
Peg	net		net			
Rex	peg		peg			
Ted	pen		pen			
Wen	pep		pep			
Wes	pet		pet			
Yeh	quell		set			
Yem	*said		sex			
Yen	sell		ten			
Zen	set		vet			
	tell		web			
	vex		well			
	wed		yell			
	well		yen			
	wet					
	yell					

*This is a sight word.

Appendix B:
Sight Words Grouped by Vowel Sounds

ă	ĕ	ĭ	ŏ	ŭ
have	said	give		a
		live		the
				of
				come
				some
				son

ā	ē	ī	ō	ū
they	be	I	go	
	me		no	
	he		so	
	she			
	we			

o͝o	o͞o	ä	er
full	do	are	her
pull	to		
put	you		

Appendix C:
Idioms

Expression	Meaning
1. to put up with it	to tolerate it (something or someone's behavior)
2. to put it off	to postpone it (something)
3. to be in the bag	to be secured or won as wished
4. to get rid of it	to discard it (something)
5. to get on with it	to do something
6. to get to it	to do something in the future
7. to get up	to awaken; to stand
8. to get with it	to understand what is happening or to be modern, up-to-date
9. to have a fit	to lose self-control (to be angry and to yell)
10. to have had it	to no longer tolerate it (a behavior or a situation)
11. to have got to	to be obligated to do something
12. to do one's bit	to make a personal contribution
13. to be fed up with	to no longer tolerate (a behavior or a situation)
14. to be up to it	to be capable of doing it (something)
15. to be on the job	to be at work
16. to be on top of it	to be in control of it (a situation)
17. to be in the red	to be in debt, to owe money
18. to be in the black	not to be in debt, not to owe money
19. to be blue	to be sad
20. to be in the pink	to be in very good health

IDIOMATIC SENTENCES: STATEMENTS AND QUESTIONS

Read:

1. Can you put up with that bad kid?
   No, I cannot put up with him.

2. Do we have to do that job on Monday, or can we put it off?
   We can put it off and do it on Tuesday.

3. She will get that job. It is in the bag.

4. That jam is bad! I will get rid of it.

5. You have to do the job. Get on with it!

6. Will you fix the bus? I will get to it if I can.

7. It is 7:15. You have to get up.

8. Dan, this hat is a big fad. Get with it!

9. He is so mad, he will have a fit.

10. She is mad! She has had it.

11. You have got to go at noon.

12. She will do her bit.

13. He is fed up with his bad job.

14. They can do it. They are up to it.

15. I am on the job at 8:00 A.M.

16. They will do it. They are on top of it.

17. She cannot get a van. She is in the red.

18. He can get a van. He is in the black.

19. She cannot go with them, so she is blue.

20. We are not ill. We are in the pink!

Write:

1. {
2. {
3. {
4. {
5. {
6. {
7. {
8. {
9. {
10. {
11. {
12. {
13. {
14. {
15. {
16. {
17. {
18. {
19. {
20. {

About the Authors

Judith S. Rubenstein received a Doctorate in Education from Harvard University and a B.A. in French from Wellesley College. Dr. Rubenstein has taught English language skills abroad and in Massachusetts (Harvard University Extension School, adult education programs, and private practice). She has published articles on various subjects in the *Boston Globe*, the *Journal of the American Medical Association, Adolescence,* and *Nature,* as well as having written, edited, and translated English and foreign language materials. As an educational consultant, Dr. Rubenstein is committed to teaching adults and children how to communicate effectively on many levels. Currently, she is creating a wide range of learning materials for speakers of English and other languages.

Janet M. Gubbay received a B.S. in sociology and anthropology from Northeastern University and studied counseling at the Northeastern Graduate School of Education. She is an experienced project leader, researcher, writer, editor, and book designer. As a writer and editor, she is committed to creating learning materials that promote personal growth and enrichment for people of all ages and backgrounds. Currently, she is writing books for children that focus on building self-esteem and encouraging independence of thought.